ELASTIC WALLS

ELASTIC WALLS

From Brooklyn to Texas and Points in Between

Eva Silverfine

Dear Aunt Joyce,
So glad you've been part of my world

love, from

Elastic Walls: From Brooklyn to Texas and Points in Between
© 2018 by Eva Silverfine

Printed in the United States of America
First Printing March 2018

Cover photo montage by Taina Litwak (http://www.litwakillustration.com); photographs by Eva Silverfine and Daniel Schwen (NYC subway station, licensed under the Creative Commons Attribution–Share Alike 2.5 Generic license).

For information, visit www.evasilverfine.com.

To all those I have found and all those I have lost along the way.

CONTENTS

Preface 1

Elastic Walls 5

   A House with Two Windows 5
   The Things That Will Fit into a House 9
   Dump with a View 13

These Are a Few of My Favorite Things 17

   I Visit Sometimes 17
   Dancing at the Academy 21
   The Gate to the Garden 24

That's the Way the Story Goes 29

   The Putting on of Water 29
   Dancing with My Father's Lady Friend..................... 33
   Far Faraway.. 37

Boardwalk Stories 41

   Riding Rockaway 41
   Pavane 43
   Roller Coasters...46

Seduction by Myth 49

   My True Love's Eyes 49
   Seduction by Myth...51
   Don't Bring Watermelon.. 54

Trying Things On 58

   Sugar Babe 58
   Suburban Heights..61
   The Day of the Dress...64

Risky Business 68

    To Bee 68
    As with All Things in ~~Life~~ Editing, Be Consistent 71
    Five Pages 74

The Tree of Life 78

    The Tree of Life 78
    Moth Genitalia I. 81
    Moth Genitalia II. 84

A Little Piece of My Heart 88

    Bluebirds, Bluebells, and Love 88
    Take Another Little Piece of My Heart 91
    Will You Come to Arkansas? 93

Where to Wear My Star of David 97

    A Confused Child 97
    The Last Bar Mitzvah 101
    Where to Wear My Star of David 103

Midlife Meanders 107

    The Grand Canyon 107
    Catharses #43 and #45 110
    Bolus #48 113

Living on the Backbone 117

    Chicken Love 117
    The One That Got Away 121
    My Friday Night Lights 125

The World Outside 128

    1968 128
    The Day the Lions Stopped Roaring 131

September 11 133

Finding Home 137
    The Smell of Fresh-Cut Grass 137
    The Boy from the Center of the Universe 140
    Tolerance Limits: August 9, 2009, 9:30 a.m. 143

Ending Chapters 146
    The Unveiling 146
    Sarah 151
    My Mother's Songbook 155

About the Author 159

PREFACE

I was perhaps eight years old, alone in the living room and dancing joyfully to Martha and the Vandellas' "Dancing in the Streets," when I said to myself, "I love this song, and I am never, ever going to forget how much I love dancing to it." This moment is the first I recall of being aware of the transitory nature of life's experiences. Perhaps this perspective is best reflected, many years later, by the animal I chose to research as a graduate student and to make the protagonist in my first attempt at a novel—the mayfly. Mayflies are known as ephemeropterans (ephemeral wings) because of their adult stage. They emerge from the water and shed their last aquatic skins to become winged insects in the terrestrial world for a day or less. Our life experiences are unique to each of us—occurring in our individual coordinates of time and place. Yet it is in these points that the essence of our lives emerge; it is within that which is transitory that we find that which is enduring.

This collection of personal narratives was written over a span of twenty-five years. They are arranged thematically rather than chronologically. As points of reference, my young sons are now young men and I still live in the Hill Country of Texas, about one hundred yards from the now-gone dwelling described herein.

Some names have been changed to protect the innocent. Still, I ask pardon of the friends and family whose privacy I have invaded.

I would like to thank those who have provided feedback over the years and iterations of various essays: James Ott, Linda Mussehl, Morton Silverfine, Debby Silverfine, Pam Hundt Reid, the many friends who commented on my web site, and the Canyon Lake Area Writers. Sara Kocek provided insightful and valuable feedback on the collection. Michael P. King generously provided guidance on self-publishing. A special thank you to Leslee Fraser, Taina Litwak, and Betty Abolafia Rosensweig for their patience and assistance with exploring and developing the cover design. And a deep appreciation to Jim Ott and Taina Litwak for their many years of encouragement.

"The Last Bar Mitzvah," "Pavane," and "The Tree of Life" were published previously in *Tiny Lights: A Journal of Personal Narrative.*

Eva Silverfine

ELASTIC WALLS

A HOUSE WITH TWO WINDOWS

I used to live in a house with two windows that looked out onto the elevated train tracks that ran above Broadway in Brooklyn. The tracks ran west to the Williamsburg Bridge, which spanned to the island of Manhattan, and east to a tangled junction known as East New York. Most of my world existed between the two closest train stations—Kosciusko Street and Gates Avenue—and the avenue that paralleled Broadway, Bushwick.

Broadway was the local shopping boulevard: around the corner was Syd, who sold us fruits and vegetables; at the corner was Marty, who once a year sold my parents wrist corsages to bestow on their three daughters after our dance recital; next door was Eunice, who cut and coiffed my mother's hair; and across the street was Lucky, to whom we took our little bit of dry cleaning. From our block we radiated out as necessity dictated—to the big grocery store and the small one, to the shoe store, to the two large movie theaters, and, after our dance recital, to the ice cream parlor where I ate lemon sherbet, fruit of the gods.

My parents owned the paint and hardware store, an essential business at which patrons had windows repaired, pipes cut and threaded, locks set, keys made, and kerosene pumped in addition to purchasing washers, screws, nails, and hammers. Advice was free. The store was old; its wooden floors were smoothed by dirt, oil, and feet. A ladder rode a rail that circumnavigated the store to give access to hardware that resided in small drawers above head height. I loved the store, even in its characteristic messiness; a community existed there.

My family lived in the two-story dwelling above the store. There was quite a diversity of rooms in that compact space, and my father had used his handiness to make the most of it. He constructed closets with built-in storage racks and a window bench for our toys; a cloths-drying rack was suspended from the ceiling by rope and pulley, as were our bikes.

I shared a large bedroom with my two sisters; our brother rated his own small bedroom. My younger sister and I slept in bunk beds; our older sister was afforded the privacy that a latticed partition provided. We each had a dresser and another personal piece of furniture nestled somewhere; mine was a vanity in the laundry alcove. It was there I kept my treasures and earliest writing.

My parents' room was separated from the girls' room by what we called the closet room—a dark, interior space I ran through with dread of the monsters that I imagined lived there. I was braver with company, but alone I could barely manage to retrieve a dress from the closet.

It was from both the girls' room upstairs and the living room below that two windows looked out onto the elevated tracks and street below. I grew up with the sound of trains in my sleep, in my play, in my homework, in my piano practice. But trains weren't the only source of street noise;

there were whistles and shouts, cars, buses, and sirens.

We lived in a neighborhood in transition—from working-class poor to out-and-out poor. My family gradually became an extreme minority, but as a kid this community defined the norm. However, our microcosm was not insulated from the larger world of the 1960s. There were riots in the streets, and although my parents' store wasn't vandalized, gates went up on the store's windows.

Eventually my parents became uneasy; the tone of the neighborhood had changed. In 1968, at the end of the school year, we moved. I cried to my friends that I would not leave them and the place I loved. But I did.

Many years later, when my father was hospitalized, I went back to my old neighborhood to check on the store for him. I was heartened to see that although the neighborhood was still extremely depressed, the store remained a vital part of the community. I went upstairs and found my first home just as I had remembered it, not one bit smaller. For all the places I have lived since, there has been none larger nor more contained. I used to live in a house with two windows that looked out; actually, I still live there.

THE THINGS THAT WILL FIT INTO A HOUSE

In 1984, thirteen years after my mother left our home in Rockaway, New York, she moved back in. Her return didn't signal reconciliation between her and my father, albeit they were on better terms than when they had separated. She moved back into the house to be useful.

A year earlier, my father had suffered nerve damage and had become quite limited in his dexterity and mobility. His lady friend of several years, Florence, saw his disability an opportunity to solidify their relationship—when he was released from the hospital, she immediately moved into the creaky, three-story bayside home. With some rearrangement of furniture, the first floor accommodated them comfortably.

Meanwhile my younger sister, with a new baby and problems of her own, also had seen the need for someone to care for our father. So she and her partner had terminated their lease and moved onto the second floor. They had more space than in their rented apartment, and there was still an intact kitchen from earlier days when the house had been divided to lodge mostly summertime residents. They even had a quasi-separate entrance.

As was characteristic, my father allowed others to make decisions for him and then claimed his innocence. The price, at least in part, was his having to listen to endless grievances from Florence against his daughter and her partner: "Why do they have to slam the door? Why do they have to run up and down the stairs all day? Why isn't he working?"

Before these rearrangements, my visits home had been welcomed respites from whatever the circumstances of my own life: I had a big house in which to roam with all the privacy I wanted; I had my family and old friends close by; and I had the ocean. Now I had to exercise constant diplomacy with Florence, and I walked on eggshells not to interfere in my sister's life. Still,

I had the third floor, left almost untouched from the time it was home to three adolescent girls. And I had the ocean.

Then my mother decided to retire early and attend law school. After years of letting my father slide on compensating her for her share of the house, she decided she wanted her money. Perhaps she distrusted Florence. In any case, she pressed my father to sell the house, and he agreed—he could no longer maintain it financially or physically. My mother returned to help with the upkeep, find a realtor, and clean out the house. Other circumstances had changed too—my sister was on her own with her child now and needed help. My mother could babysit while my sister returned to work. So my mother moved onto the third floor. There were remnants of a kitchen there too.

When I went home to visit, my mother, who had been using my old bedroom as her own, graciously returned it to me. If I closed the door, I could pretend to find some peace. It was illusory. I bounced between my mother's floor, my sister's floor, and my father and Florence's floor. Every dinner was a tactical decision.

"Florence put in some turkey legs and made fresh (canned) fruit salad" meant I was to eat with my father and Florence. Before my first sip of morning coffee I had to announce, "Sarah asked me to eat with her tonight"; or, more cryptically for dining with my mother, "Don't worry about me for dinner." Every hour home I had my choice of insanity. I was there for just a week or so at a time. My sister was there for the duration.

Seemingly fixed, the walls of a house are really elastic, accommodating all sorts of things inside. There must be a limit to their elasticity, though—a tensile strength—when the house becomes a place of stress instead of refuge; when there is discord between the first, second, and third floors; when there are three kitchens in which to eat.

Within eight months my mother went on to law school, my father sat uneasy with his decision to sell the house but held he had no choice, and my sister found an apartment in the neighborhood. Now my visits home were to help clean out closets, sort things, and move furniture.

I miss that seaside house. Through all its history, it was the place of family. I carry its remnants around with me from dwelling to dwelling. Like a hermit crab transferring its anemones from old shell to new, I arrange my old possessions in new places. I am still waiting, though, for a house that fits me as well.

DUMP WITH A VIEW

"Isn't that a stitch?" laughed one old friend when we told her of our new, modest home. "Bring it along when you come to visit," suggested another. Swallowing East Coast pride and prejudices, my husband and I bought a doublewide when we moved to Texas in 1994.

There are some real fine features to our doublewide: space is used efficiently and there are plenty of electrical outlets. We even have two bathrooms for the first time in our married life. On the other hand, in our fifteen-year-old Pinewood every faucet drips, not every door closes, and squirrels have made the crawl space their own.

With the same prescience with which I had declared when we moved to urban Maryland, "I don't want to live anywhere near this intersection"—and soon ended up only blocks away—so I asked my husband when we happened to drive by what became our home, "Why can't we find a dump like that?"

Our dump, you see, has a view. From our moderately level perch the land falls away at a forty-five-degree angle into one of the many canyons that characterize the area known as the Devil's Backbone. Our vista includes some of the yet uncluttered slopes of the Texas Hill Country. They are dry hills. Clumps of dark trees, mostly junipers, contrast with the lighter green of the often-parched herbaceous growth. The ground is accented with the gray of Late Cretaceous limestone. The sky, of course, is big.

Vultures and ravens ride the air currents above the canyons, and wrens nest under the house. I have heard the raw call of a male roadrunner and watch turkeys court in the yard. My son has held an injured male painted bunting in his hands, and the endangered golden-cheeked warbler comes to our birdbath. We stop for Texas alligator lizards lumbering across the gravel road with their thick, heavy tails and bright blue tongues and take joy in every fence lizard, skink, and anole we see. Snakes are viewed with thrill and caution. Besides the rather pedestrian foxes, raccoons, possums, armadillos, and deer in the yard, we have had two spotted skunks try to move in, and a truly treasured ringtail spent a fat winter subsidized by a sack of cat food left in the shed. Garden spiders weave their intricate orbs under the doublewide's eaves, butterflies search for nectar among the wildflowers, tarantulas are sighted infrequently, scorpions are encountered frequently. Only fire ants are looked upon with scorn.

We are fifteen miles out of town—about a twenty-minute drive unless I got stuck behind a horse trailer. In Maryland, a twenty-minute drive might have gotten me the four miles to work; now it has given me the quiet for which I always have longed.

Moving into my new home wasn't only about city versus country living, or East versus West. The transition was more about those laughs I heard when I told my friends about our doublewide. The transition was about my internalized sense of home—a multistoried, old house with delightful nooks and crannies. It was that quaint old house, full of nuances, which breathes a history, that I always imagined as me, as my home.

THESE ARE A FEW OF MY FAVORITE THINGS

I VISIT SOMETIMES

I eat from my grandparents' dishes. I sleep in one of their beds. I store my clothes in their dresser. I surround myself with old family things, as if the possessions themselves continue the family lore.

I sometimes visit my grandparents in my mind's eye. I race up the dark stairs of their two-family, semi-attached home in Brooklyn. When I open the door, I am supposed to smell the wonderful aroma of chicken soup, top of the rib, and egg barley, but memories fall short of the true experience. We, four children and my parents, invade my father's parents' home. Grandpa—short, barrel-chested, and energetic—is bustling around the kitchen. He has a snack for us of chopped eggs on crackers and precious Coca-Cola. We throw our coats down in one bedroom and quietly enter the other to kiss Grandma hello. Grandma, with down-turned blue eyes, is most often resting, already worn from her battle with breast cancer. My parents stay to talk with her, and we children return to the large, sunny kitchen for our snack. As I eat, I study the decals of butlers and maids that adorn the cabinets. Grandpa serves us, yells at us, and gives us little behind-his-back kicks in the *toches* as signs of his affection.

Soon dinner is served in the dining room. As I enter I look up with an admixture of fear and reverence of the dead at the framed photo and Purple Heart. I imagine the uncle I will never know, how life with him might have been. If Grandma is feeling well enough she comes to the table—sometimes to eat, sometimes just to visit. I still remember pieces of conversation, conversation in a Yiddish–English construction that defined their Brooklynese and that haphazardly colored my youthful perceptions of the world.

Well before dinner is over, I am eyeing the bowl that later will be filled with chocolate. Next to it are the four molded figurines from St. Petersburg, Florida—Ben with a banjo, Lem with an accordion, Clem with a fiddle, and Pete with a penny whistle. Over the afternoon I will arrange and rearrange them. They still keep me company today.

After dinner the children are left to their own devices while the grownups visit. We greedily eat the chocolate but at a pace at which we won't be chastised. We compete for the comics from the Sunday newspaper. We dig into the junk drawer and pull out marbles, coloring books, and balls and jacks. We sit with the comics and toys on the floor of the living room where there hangs, in a large, gilded frame, a colorized photograph of our glamorous aunt from her days as a chorus girl. If Grandma is well enough, we visit with her briefly one by one. Sometimes we join her on the front porch. To get there we go through a small room used mostly for storage but having the mystique of being where "the boys" slept—young men passing through Brooklyn during World War II.

When our father and grandfather go to the basement or garage to check on "things," we follow them. From the garage we pull out the old scooter, go cart, and tall tricycle and ride up and down the driveway shared by neighboring houses. We play handball with a Pensy Pinky. Sometimes we go into the little garden space to weed or plant flowers.

When it is time to leave, Grandpa follows us and fills our car with gas at the corner station. He works there a few hours a day—not too far from home but out in the world.

As my grandparents get older, we bring cold cuts from a kosher deli and often eat with Grandpa only; Grandma spends more time in bed under the influence of morphine. We children bring our homework or quiet hobbies; the toys in the junk drawer no longer interest us.

Until I was fifteen years old I visited my grandparents, Gussie and Jack, practically every Sunday. Then, on the same day, they were both taken to the hospital, and on separate floors they both died of cancer within a month of one another. My grandfather had hidden his illness in order to care for my grandmother.

I love when a smell or sound reminds me of my grandparents' home. Sometimes I dream of them or the house, and I savor the dream in the morning. These dreams are the best visits memory allows.

DANCING AT THE ACADEMY

There was a time when I was going to be a ballerina; there was a time when dancing spoke for my soul. But I don't dance much anymore.

I started dancing when I was four years old. Dance immediately became my art—my body cooperated, I understood the rhythm of the music and the concept of practice, I relished the attention of my dance instructor, I adored dressing in costume, and I had no inhibitions about performing. I loved the stage.

And what a stage! Although I attended a small, local dance school in an impoverished neighborhood, our dance recitals were held in the splendor of a lavish theater completed in 1908, the Brooklyn Academy of Music. However, by the 1960s the Academy, located in a neighborhood then deemed dangerous by many, fell out of favor.

A true theater with a large stage, full curtains, ornate staircases, a balcony and boxes, worn yet plush seats, and dressing rooms was ours for two nights—dress rehearsal and recital. During the dress rehearsal, between my numbers, I raced to the theater's balcony to watch others perform or danced the Alley Cat with my sisters and friends in the dressing room; during the recital I waited for each of my numbers with great anticipation.

In bright red lipstick and with a large black beauty mark beside my mouth—my mother's touch—I went on stage in my glittery costumes with an excitement that could not be rivaled by anything else in my life. I sang, I danced, I basked in the applause.

After the recital, my parents gave me and my sisters wrist corsages and took us to our neighborhood ice cream parlor. There, on our rare visit, I ate sherbet, the most sublime delicacy in my culinary experience.

Those special nights lasted until I was eleven, when my dance instructor died in an auto accident. My mother found other nearby dance studios for me, but they were businesses, not schools. By the time I found a good teacher on my own, my body had become too awkward and my focus too diffuse to pursue dancing seriously. By college I readily gave up dance.

My dancing renaissance occurred when I joined a dance club in my twenties. Too late to become a dancer but not too late to learn, I began to understand some of the lessons I had never truly understood before—how to gain balance, strength, and grace by lifting the inner axis between my pelvis and chest and how, during each and every rehearsal, to dance as if I were performing because doing so was the only means to performing well. I also learned that there was a place in my life for something to which I had once aspired to excel and now aspired only to enjoy.

It was also at this time that dance became the voice of my soul. Dream after dream had me dancing in symbolism so rich it propelled me forward. I danced on the streets of New York City,

I danced with the children with whom I had grown up, and I floated on air once I achieved the syncopated rhythm.

I continued to dance—at parties, in dreams, and around my apartment on Saturday afternoons—but eventually I no longer pursued a formal outlet for my movement.

Now I rarely dance. Sometimes I feel a sense of loss because dancing is no longer part of my life or dreams. Once in a while, when I turn on music, my young sons dash into the room, and we dance about frenetically. For now, this is enough.

THE GATE TO THE GARDEN

"Do you know the combination?" my husband asked as he handed me an old brass lock he had dug out of a drawer in the shed. As the lock arrived in my palm, my spirit lifted, a rush of sweet memory flooding me. I quickly dialed the combination and popped the lock open: "Zero, zero, zero, zero."

My father, a locksmith, had set the combination. The lock is from our old garage in Rockaway, the door of which could have been kicked in quicker than the combination set. But the lock was a deterrent, and my father made the combination easy to remember—and, I imagine to his mind, too obvious to guess. Holding the lock made me think of the lyric from *Porgy and Bess*, "Folks with plenty of plenty, they got a lock on their door, afraid somebody's gonna rob them while they're out making more, what for?"

It would be disingenuous to pretend I do not secure my possessions. The reality of theft and greater perils came to me by the time I was ten, when my parents joined the ranks of other store owners and put up gates across the windows and entrance to their store in Brooklyn.

Quickly the gates became a part of our everyday life. My father would close and lock the gates at the end of the business day. In the summer, when we children were allowed to stay outside in the evenings, we unlocked and relocked the gates as we passed through.

Many years later, when I returned from my first visit to the Hill Country of Texas, I kept dreaming of large gates and fences. I was unaccustomed to this Texas aesthetic, shared by those who could afford only a humble metal gate to those who could build elaborate entrance edifices. By then I was accustomed to the largely unfenced East Coast countryside.

I have since learned that farmers originally erected fences to protect their crops from livestock, but by the 1880s fences began to be used to keep livestock in as well. Since then, fences, and their gates, have evolved. There are fences to show ownership akin to dominion; fences to keep out the uninvited and unwanted; high fences to keep wildlife in because it is seen as owned property; high fences to keep the wildlife out because it destroys vegetation; and, still, fences to keep livestock in or out. Entrance gates, in their composition, typically establish the owners' financial status. Sometimes the gate outshines the abode within.

There was one fence in my early life, though, that along with its multiple gates set apart a world of immeasurable value. From a noisy, dirty, concrete world I passed through these gates and stepped onto a path that seemed to me the yellow brick road through the Land of Oz: the Brooklyn

Botanic Garden. The gates to the Garden were locked at night, but in the morning visitors were allowed to pass freely (and years ago, literally so) into this priceless paradise. In the midst of an urban environment this oasis provided me a haven and a glimpse of the world that beckoned me to its reaches. It was a world of green, of flowering trees and shrubs, of perennials and annuals, of lily ponds and streams, of fruits and vegetables. There were dragonflies, bees, and butterflies, birds and squirrels, fish and tadpoles. There, from a generation of female horticulturalists and botanists whose exceptionalism I didn't recognize at the time, I learned to turn soil, plant seeds, pull weeds, and tend my crops. There I found beauty that reached beyond what humans could create. At a young age I recognized the world held within the Garden offered me a serenity that filled an inherent need. The fence and gates protected the Garden, but they also reminded us that we were entering a world to be cherished.

The old combination lock spends most of its time in a drawer. Its use is occasional and transitory. There are no gates to our little piece of Texas.

THAT'S THE WAY THE STORY GOES

THE PUTTING ON OF WATER

My father owned a paint and hardware store. More than a vendor, he was someone who worked with his hands, hands unsteadied by coffee, hands with long, dirty fingernails. He fixed broken things, patched them back together to make them work again. And if he couldn't make them work, he stored them for their parts.

My father was a man of routine. Over the years he accommodated himself to the changes life brought him by finding a routine that fit the circumstances. With a routine, one can adapt.

For many years my family lived in the apartment above the store. Six days a week my father would go downstairs at 7 a.m., walk the two watchdogs around the block, and, once back in the store, put on a pot of coffee in the richly stained vacuum pot. He would chain the rolls of wire out in front, set up his cash register, and then spend the day selling his wares and giving advice. During quiet times, he would repair windows, set locks, and cut and thread pipes. At 6:30 p.m., he would roll in the wire, take most of the cash out of the register, and walk the dogs. He would be up for dinner by 7 p.m., walk the dogs again at 10:30, and then watch the 11:00 news. On Sundays we went to visit his parents. Once a year we went camping for a week. We had a camping routine too.

When I was twelve, my family moved to a house in Rockaway, which was a forty-or-so-minute drive from the store. The change was easy to accommodate. My father left for the store earlier, returned home later, and would often bring home one of the dogs for a visit with the family. There were more things to fix now that he owned a big, old house, but he could go fishing on summer evenings in the bay across the street.

We continued to visit his parents on Sunday and went camping for a week during the summer.

Then changes began to come quickly. My mother took a part-time job. My father's mother was losing her long battle with cancer. My mother began to lose weight and bleach her hair. Both my father's parents died of cancer within a month of one another. My mother started to come home late at night. My mother had a boyfriend. My mother moved out.

My father's life—my family's life—broke in a way that could not be fixed. The remaining parts regrouped and reassigned responsibilities. We found new routines to accommodate us to the changes; now I know these accommodations did not suffice to repair the damage.

For my father, routines were like rituals— rituals that, if followed consistently and faithfully, would lead one to prescribed outcomes. He had worked steadily, provided for his family, maintained his home, remained faithful to both his wife and his parents—yet the outcome was wrong.

For some years there was no true routine. Like usable, stored parts, remnants of rituals held my father together. He continued to work and provide for his children, but he was lost.

Then my father salvaged himself. He met Florence, and over the years they developed a new routine. At first it was the Saturday night dance together, then the Sunday afternoon fishing, and soon the midweek bowling date. Eventually there were the two-family holiday dinners. By the time his children were all out of the house, my father and Florence spent most of their evenings and weekends together. When he became disabled, Florence moved in, and a new routine ensued. As my father aged and his limitations grew, his routine had less and less variety.

My father used to drink a cup of coffee every night as he watched the 11:00 news. Shortly before it started, he would rise and say in his Brooklynese, "I'm puttin' on the water. Anybody wan' anything?" And then we would all drink coffee together. It wasn't until I went out into the world that I realized that, unlike my family, drinking coffee at night caused me insomnia. It wasn't until I went out into the world on my own did I realize the rituals of my youth were largely the idiosyncrasies of a small, fragile clan.

DANCING WITH MY FATHER'S LADY FRIEND

My father and his lady friend were caught up in disco fever during their early dating. Disco appealed to my father—the steps were laid out at a time nothing else was. My father appealed to his lady friend—albeit he had four adolescent children, he was a familiar vintage and was willing to learn the dance.

When my father first brought Florence home, everyone was on good behavior. We would sit around the living room and have pleasant chats. We would all gently gang up on my father and tease him about his bad eating and dressing habits. With time, Florence would stay for meals, although she would always protest: "I'll just have some lettuce and tomato; I'm kosher, you know." We then would prepare tuna fish salad or something else she could eat. Her daughter, in her mid-twenties, began to visit too. Over the first few years we were smoothly gliding toward becoming a comfortable extended family.

I suspect the definition of family became the crux of the matter—that Florence expected marriage to be part of the natural progression of the dance.

The friction surfaced with a present. Florence insisted she had always wanted a toy race track as a child, so one holiday we children gave her one. We were informed later that Florence felt we were making fun of her. We worked harder at giving her respectful gifts and interpreting her desires, but we found it increasingly difficult to maintain our position in the corp. We learned Florence knew something about everything. She was an expert on surgery because her deceased husband had spent a lot of time in the hospital; an expert on diet and nutrition because her parents had owned a fruit and vegetable stand; and an expert on education because her daughter was a teacher.

Then the next movement began. Florence began to develop intense dislikes for couples with which she and my father had been friendly. First they stopped going to their Saturday night dances, and eventually they dropped from their bowling league. The last frontier for Florence became my father's children.

My father began to visit Florence at her home more often. Our conversations with her became more restricted. We wanted to keep peace for my father's sake, but there was no clear path. Florence didn't want peace: she wanted victory, which she had choreographed as a *pas de trois*— our father, her, and her daughter.

Once we were all well into our adulthood, time spent as a family became quite limited. Every Chanukah–Christmas my older sister would host a family gathering, and every year Florence threatened my father she wouldn't attend. She always did, though, because worse than going was my father going without her. She would arrive and turn on "the game" loud enough so she could hear it over the voices of the crowd. When asked, she would request "a Bloody Mary with only the slightest trace of vodka" and then assess, "This drink is so weak; I can't even taste any vodka." As my sister set out copious amounts of food for the gathering, Florence would worry that there would be nothing for her to eat. Yet every year there was a sumptuous plate of smoked salmon and whitefish, cream cheese, fine bread, and garnishes.

When my father was hospitalized for degeneration of the vertebrae, Florence became hysterical. "The doctors say he'll never walk again!" she proclaimed, although the doctors had said nothing of the sort. When I queried one morning what time she would be at the hospital—yes, I was trying to avoid her—she told my father I had told her she shouldn't visit him anymore. Luckily I lived out of town, so I could wear the cloak of villain without much effort on my part.

When my father was released from the hospital, Florence moved into the family home with him. Now when we visited, we were intruders in their world. Once my father sold the house, they moved into Florence's apartment together. Visits to my father at their apartment were rare and brief. There were still the periodic family get togethers: everyone spent a few hours together, ate a lot of good food, and accepted this as the new normal.

You never know on what note the dance will end. My father kept company with his lady friend as long as he was married to my mother.

FAR FARAWAY

"So he went off to Mexico to find himself, and his wife ended up with the house and the two kids," the realtor told me in explaining the history of the property. "You know the way the story goes. . . ."

Yes, sort of. Except it wasn't my father; it was my mother. And it wasn't Mexico; it was Far Rockaway—about five miles down the road. They were a far five miles though.

In the early 1970s, my mother left her husband and four children to go find herself. I have vivid memories of the year she worked up to leaving. She had taken a part-time job at the post office. Having been heavy since she started having children almost 20 years earlier, she began to lose weight. She took up smoking cigarettes. As she thinned, she began to bleach her hair blond. She read psychology books and books on relationships. She listened to The Carpenters sing Burt Bacharach's "(They Long to Be) Close to You" and played it over and over again on the piano. Often angry with us she would say, "What have you done for me lately?"

Blaming society for channeling her into marriage and motherhood and discouraging her from a career, blaming her husband and children for her failure to find fulfillment and contentment, blaming her husband for a lack of emotional involvement in their relationship, she left. Her boyfriend helped her move a few things from our house to their apartment in Far Rockaway.

Early on I had been frightened by the changes in her behavior; she was betraying the family. But by time she left, I was relieved. She had vacillated between being angry or absent. Both inflicted pain.

Once she left, the rest of us coalesced. Chores were reassigned. We ate better because my brother turned out to be a much better cook than our mother. I did laundry, my older sister did the grocery shopping, and we all cleaned house. But all was not as harmonious as we tried to maintain. My older sister was burdened with family responsibilities that conflicted with pursuing her own young life. My brother's temper flared. My younger sister was largely ignored. She retreated into her world of school friends and solitary games. After one year we gave up the idea of family vacation—it was just days of arguments and tears.

My mother was scarce for a few years, in touch but not frequently. Gradually her anger subsided. Perhaps we were no longer keeping her from what she really wanted; perhaps she realized she wasn't sure what it was. On some level we children accepted her reasons for leaving. I visited her a few times in Far Rockaway and met her boyfriend. They were living the life of adults without children—they traveled frequently, went to theater, ate out.

Eventually my mother wanted freedom and independence from her boyfriend too, and she claimed them. She moved alone to Manhattan. It was then that my mother came back into our lives more fully. Besides the fact that she was no longer married to my father, it was almost as if she had never left. But that is not true.

My friends used to marvel at how well I understood and accepted my mother's reasons for leaving, how little anger I expressed toward her, how well my family managed from the outset without her. Yet the consequences of having my foundation rocked, of being blamed and left, are not so far faraway.

BOARDWALK STORIES

RIDING ROCKAWAY

My ten-speed Raleigh–Carleton Supercourse was olive green with purple handlebar tape. I bought it the spring I was fifteen, in preparation for a three-week cycling trip in Maine.

Oh, I was so cool riding my sleek bike, speeding along city streets, leaning into turns at just the right angle. I was never without a screwdriver and adjustable wrench in the black leather pouch that hung behind the seat: I could tighten my brakes, align my wheels, adjust my derailleur. This liberating mode of transportation was so alluring that my two best friends soon followed suit. We rode the streets of Rockaway together—to one another's homes, to the movie theater and pizzeria, to the end of the peninsula. We would stop smartly whenever we saw someone we knew.

After returning from Maine that summer, when there were no longer hills to ascend or thirty-mile days to press, I would cruise the streets of the neighborhood looking for the proverbial action of adolescence. The evenings were the best time to ride—bathed by cool ocean breezes and incandescent lights. Several mornings each week I would craftily dodge car doors and buses on a ten-mile trip down Flatbush Avenue to my job at the Brooklyn Botanic Garden. That first summer I became a veteran bike rider.

The following fall my friends and I made weekend bike trips. Once, we left Rockaway, rode across Brooklyn and the tip of Manhattan, traveled across New York Bay on the Staten Island Ferry, and ended our voyage at the Staten Island Zoo. Then, in the rain, we rode all the way back again. We were empowered. Gradually, though, new social horizons appeared: at sixteen, I fell in love. I would ride five miles down the wooden-plank boardwalk—terrible for my bike's tires—

just to pass his house. Another spring and summer passed. My trusted bike served me well. But then, in the fall, there was a new boyfriend, and he had a car. My bike was often left behind.

Over the years I moved my bike from state to state as I toured the nation via college and graduate school, but the new streets were never quite as inviting as those of Rockaway. Eventually I left the bike behind in a friend's shed in North Carolina—there was just no more room in my car. I always planned to go back for it, but I never managed to make that trip.

I still think of my Raleigh–Carton Supercourse, leaning against the wall of the old wood shed, only slightly rusted, forever holding its early promise of self-propelled freedom.

PAVANE

Comfortably my mother sat down at the piano and opened the book that laid on the music rest. Comfortably she began to play the music, page by page. As always her fingers landed a bit heavily on the keys, but still, I admired her facility at sight-reading music. After playing several pieces, she played the opening refrain of Ravel's *Pavane pour une infante défunte*.

The notes resonated deep within me. I knew the music well. It was the piece with which I had auditioned to the High School of Music and Art. My music teacher chose it. I played the French horn, an instrument that required a good ear, technical skill, and self-confidence. The piece was difficult; it started on a two-and-one-half count high D. The technical difficulty mixed with my nervousness led to my playing a broken D at the audition. I barely could complete the first refrain. My judges were sympathetic; they suggested I instead play some scales. For reasons of which I have never been sure—although I suspect it had something to do with mentioning, when asked, that my mother's cousin was a well-known bassoonist—I was accepted.

When my mother finished the piece I asked, "Do you remember my practicing that on the horn?"

"No," she replied.

How could she not remember, I wondered. How could she not remember? I practiced every day, just as she had taught me and my siblings to do from the time she began to teach each of us the piano. My obedience to that lesson made me the music teacher's model student.

Where had she been while I was practicing? Gone. I played *Pavane* the year my mother was in the process of leaving us. Even when she was home, she was focused on her inner turmoil and her life outside our home. So she did not hear me practice *Pavane*, nor did she hear my band perform in the spring. She wasn't there to see my dance recital or to see me play the lead in the junior high school play. I did these things because I loved dance and music and I loved to perform— loves that my mother had engendered in me. She moved out by the end of the school year.

The summer after she left was the summer of my bicycle trip through Maine. I traveled with nine other adolescents and an "adult" barely out of college. We were all out of our accustomed context of friends and family, and a social hierarchy was quickly established. Falling somewhere in the middle, I was exposed on that trip, vulnerable to the unkindness of some of my peers. The erosion of self-confidence gathers momentum. One day, speeding down a hill, I narrowly missed hitting gravel. In fright I cried out, "Mommy!", a cry that would escape me, with embarrassment, into my adulthood. Then I thought, "I don't have a 'mommy' anymore."

A high, mournful D starts a refrain that I could not play but that still plays my soul. Childhood was over that summer. *Défunte*.

ROLLER COASTERS

In the first few weeks after I moved halfway across the country to Texas, I dreamt of family— husband and child, parents and siblings, in- laws—on various beaches facing towering waves. I have dreamt of families and homes on sand for years.

When my family moved to Rockaway, that oh- so-un-city spit of sand at the end of the A-train line, compared with Brooklyn it seemed too tame. But with time I learned to appreciate its seclusion—summer nights with friends on the boardwalk after daytime visitors had left; fall and winter walks on empty beaches; springtime bike rides along quiet streets that held the promise of chance encounters with acquaintances.

It was soon after my mother left that my siblings and I began to leave one by one. At first it was an innocent summer away, but the groundwork was laid for the dissolution. Within a few years only my younger sister remained with our father in our creaky, old house.

Dreams of living on a beach became my almost-too-perfect metaphor for the precarious nature of homes and families and the transient nature of our lives' bearings. In my adolescence I dreamt of living on the exposed beach, building shelters in the sand, and being threatened by huge waves. Yet for years the home in Rockaway remained the place of family, where we gathered and found comfort in a shared history, where I found refuge when needed. Eventually, though, the house was sold, my father moved to an apartment in Brooklyn, and my younger sister to an apartment in Rockaway.

One day my sister called to tell me that she and her husband were moving to California. I went home to see them before the move. And again, too perfect a metaphor, that weekend, from my sister's balcony, we watched as the amusement park, Playland, was demolished.

Built on sand, Rockaway is a community not so much unlike other ones. Lives are lived and passed, and memories are eroded away by time and change. Eras are washed away with the inevitable passage of time—the whole becomes fragments and eventually grains. We pass on things—trinkets, houses, businesses, and myths—our goal to create a permanent presence.

I miss the sense of home that once existed. I miss a seemingly permanent place. Eroded by one wave, the sands shifted forever.

There are no traces left of my family having once resided in Rockaway.

SEDUCTION BY MYTH

MY TRUE LOVE'S EYES

I fell in love for the first time with a guy that looked like Bob Dylan, dressed life Bob Dylan, and knew the lyrics of every Bob Dylan song. Jacob had a sharp mind, was quick with words, and had gained respect among his peers for his insightfulness. Unlike Bob Dylan, though, Jacob was only seventeen, and I squirmed uneasily but invisibly when Jacob applied Dylan's lyrics of women to me.

Somewhere between fourteen and fifteen I had "blossomed" from a petit, undeveloped girl into a well-endowed—*zaftig*—adolescent. By the time I was sixteen, males described me as a woman and an "earth mother." I was nothing of the sort, but I didn't tell them this. I tried to be what they wanted me to be. I made the mistake of thinking "older" males knew more than I, knew better than I.

My romance with Jacob lasted only a few months—its course had already been laid out in Dylan songs. At the time of our break up I had no idea what had happened, how *I* had failed. Now I know that Jacob didn't have a clue about relationships either; he didn't know what made their substance.

Since then there have been other boys and men in my life. I became a woman under their influence and regardless of their influence. With them I learned about relationships. With most of them I remain friends.

Ten years after I had last seen Jacob, while I was home visiting family, he got in touch. We met on the boardwalk. He no longer looked like Dylan; he was a bit too chubby. The fine line he had straddled between brilliance and craziness had leaned toward the latter. He wanted to show me something, and I agreed to go with him. I soon realized my mistake: he planned to take me on a several hour drive to Montauk Point. I was relieved when he turned his car around and took me home when I declined to go.

Still, I thank Jacob for reminding me that day of who I wanted to be when I was sixteen—a writer, not the scientist I was studying to become. Now a woman, I clearly saw myself in my old true love's eyes.

SEDUCTION BY MYTH

I stood on the sandy shore, searching the horizon. I was waiting—for something, for someone. And then an Aegean vessel appeared and rode the waves to shore. He disembarked—a man of large stature and masculine countenance. But I was not a maiden easily seduced by exteriors.

Although I dwelled on the fringes of the marketplace, I had walked to the beach where those with greater wealth dwelt. Reasonably attired, I was easily swept along with the group who greeted the rowdy crew ashore. This is how I came to be in the company of this man of good breeding and status. I must forego modesty to say that he may have noticed me—a young maiden, of pleasing countenance and form. Still his attention was drawn by my words, as mine to his: always I have been seduced by words.

His crew were his companions, all embracing their adventurous travels. The drunken men were speaking of the inherent goodness of the wine when I had the courage to ask, "Do the gods love what is good or is the good, good because the gods love it?" His mates preferred to revel than discuss, but he left them to engage me in discourse.

His ship left in the morning, but he returned many times and sought my company. He took me to wondrous feasts among his companions. Our courtship was slowly paced, and when he went abroad, we exchanged long letters full of eloquent flourishes—not only of our daily lives but our readings and our deeper ponderings. He gave me views of the world that were largely foreign to my station.

Reality: Jason's vessel was his parents' 1960s vintage Cadillac that could seat seven or eight in pre-seat-belt days. And his journey was from his family's brownstone in Park Slope in Brooklyn across the bay to his family's beach house in the wealthiest part of Rockaway. And the first time we met I had macraméd his boot laces together while sitting around his parent-free beach house with hordes of other teenagers. But we were at the beach, and we did speak of philosophy, and, both lovers of the written word, when he returned to college we did exchange long letters imitating diverse writing styles and pondering philosophical intrigues. That first summer he introduced me to his prep school friends, and over subsequent visits I met his private college friends. He took me to feast at his family's landmark Brooklyn restaurant, where at a large, round, white-linen-covered table his elegant Greek mother, dressed in black, sat with her siblings and their spouses.

But as in most adolescent relationships, the more time we had together, the more bad habits we developed. I was jealous of the time he spent with friends; he became insecure about our relationship when we were apart.

His visits grew in duration, and at first we reveled in our time together. But I began to desire to voyage beyond my own borders too. He would rather I stay ashore, but I could not. I was too young to settle without seeing more of the world. While he was at sea, I found my own vessel and sailed away.

DON'T BRING WATERMELON

"I don't like watermelon," Katherine told me when I presented my gifts.

I felt like my mother, inappropriately schlepping a watermelon, a bottle of New York State wine, and a bouquet of cockscomb from the Union Square farmers' market in lower Manhattan to this affluent Westchester County suburb north of the city. The watermelon and wine were put aside, a vase was found for the flowers, and they were displayed on a side cupboard.

I was visiting an old friend, his recent bride, and their newborn.

I met David when I was sixteen and we were starting our freshman year of college. I found him to be the most elegant person I had ever known. He was well educated, articulate, creative, multilingual, at home in the United States and

Europe. He was from a family of accomplished musicians and was one himself. Still, he had no airs or pretensions and relished the sensuous of life's mundane experiences.

At the end of our freshman year, David and I both transferred to the University of Chicago, where we ended up living in the same dorm. We spent a great deal of time together, and our friendship grew. Although we seemed to talk about everything, we never talked directly about our relationship. I did not know if David wanted a relationship other than our platonic one, and I would not risk rejection or our friendship to ask. Instead, I filled in the blanks. Early on I either had seen or convinced myself that David was attracted to girls more sophisticated, more refined, than myself. I was a working-class girl from Brooklyn who had her rough edges barely smoothed.

I left Chicago after one year. I was young, and the University of Chicago was a grim environment. Also, I didn't know how to fix friendships I had managed to damage that year.

I continued college in New Hampshire. Over the years, from New Hampshire to Virginia to

North Carolina and beyond, David and I have remained in loose touch. In our later twenties circumstances found us both in New York City— he was living there, playing and studying music; I was visiting often because my father was ill. We enjoyed the time we spent together and were closer than we had been in years. I again experienced all the things I loved about David.

On one trip, I shared with him my self-revelation—although I had just completed a Master's in science, my true ambition was to be a writer. I told him about the novel I had started, the novels I planned to write, and he responded with enthusiasm. His support, his belief in me, was priceless. It legitimized me. He had that power. Unique to this relationship, I had placed David on a pedestal.

David and my New York visits tapered off. My home in Rockaway had been emptied in preparation for sale. But more significantly, David had met the woman he would marry—a woman who was well educated and well cultured—and I had no place in his new life.

I cannot say who I was, who I might have been, in David's eyes; I can only conjecture. In the absence of dialogue, I infused his vision of me with my own insecurities, my own shortcomings. Although I still feel my own rough edges on those rare occasions that I see David, I now have ceded his vision of me, whatever it may have been, or is, to him. I cherish those instances, however fleeting, when I feel we recapture the connection we had all those years ago.

A few years after the watermelon visit, David and Katherine had another child, and I visited them in their newly purchased home. This time I had brought some fine cheeses and crackers. As I unpacked them, I asked Katherine for a plate to lay out my offering. "Oh," she said, "David can't eat those. He's discovered he's lactose intolerant."

TRYING THINGS ON

SUGAR BABE

He appeared as if a knight in shining armor, not that he was what I would have ever imagined my knight to be—with his wrestler's thick neck and cauliflowered ears. He made bad jokes, picked me up and spun me around, and took amusement in the everyday. Most importantly, he didn't take me too seriously. With his slightly southern accent and rowdy ways he rescued me from the somber outlook that I was embracing.

What did Lyle see in me? I essentially appeared from nowhere, was available, and was young and in need of someone to help me grow up. Lyle could not resist someone in need of parenting.

Lyle worked as a carpenter and drove a panel truck in which the heater didn't work. He lived in a run-down house with two guys he knew from high school. He also happened to be the older brother of a good friend of mine from college; I knew him before we ever met.

Within months we went off to Texas together; Lyle had a job lined up in Abilene. We moved into a trailer outside town and created a life, albeit somewhat sparse. We worked, learned to play tennis, ate pie and drank iced tea (the only kind in Texas) in local cafes, and explored the countryside, taking pictures of cows and identifying wildflowers. And we talked, we always talked.

Over the years I learned a lot from Lyle, and he was a ready mentor. I learned how to flex my biceps and perform basic car maintenance because our old vehicles were always breaking; I learned not to pay on a job until it is finished; I learned that life is not fair; I learned that anger is a nonconstructive emotion and I had a hell of a lot of it; and I learned that one's greatest commodity is one's integrity.

Lyle and I shared a number of homes. He followed me to New Hampshire when I returned to college to finish my undergraduate degree. He didn't stay long—the scarcity of work, the cold weather, and better prospects down south called him back to Virginia. I spent summers with him there, and when I graduated I moved there, and we set up house for the next two years.

Lyle and I shared dreams together. We would drive through the Virginia countryside and imagine renovating an old, abandoned church into a home; we would play guitar and imagine becoming accomplished enough to perform; we each imagined how we would become what we wanted for ourselves.

I don't think Lyle and I were ever in love; instead we were companions in exploration. With time our dreams began to diverge, or, perhaps, they became a wedge. He wanted to pursue being a successful businessman and having a family. I, more uncertain in my aspirations, decided to attend graduate school. And perhaps we both wanted to be in love.

I left for North Carolina; Lyle remained in Virginia, struggling to build a business. We visited, but our relationship was already in dissolution.

When I think of Lyle now, I see him with his shoulders hunched up around his ears to brace himself against a cold for which he is not properly dressed; he is standing over a broken-down car and wearing the lopsided grin that speaks of finding humor in his situation. And I hear him singing one of the songs he used to play on guitar:

"Sugar babe, what's the matter with you?
You don't love me like you used to do.
Sugar babe, it's all over now."

SUBURBAN HEIGHTS

Having finished my undergraduate degree, I moved to Northern Virginia. Lyle and I were going to play house. He had a small construction business, and I found an entry-level job in the county government. We rented a very suburban dwelling with trees in fall foliage. Looking out onto the other suburban homes from the big bay window in the breakfast nook conjured up my worst fears of housewifedom.

We arranged what little bit of furniture we had, trimmed bushes and raked leaves in the yard, and took in a stray, pregnant cat. Then, we almost took in Lyle's grandfather.

Grandpa had moved from upper New York State to his son's home in Virginia. He had grown afraid of being alone—of his failing health and local hooligans. He brought with him some furnishings and a long life's mementos. There was no room in his son's home for all this, so Lyle invited him to store his belongings in the large basement of our rented home.

Grandpa would take the bus from his son's house to ours to sort through his possessions. When I came home from work, he just barely had arrived. He showed me vases and scraps of paper; whatever I admired, he gave me. I learned to keep such appreciations to myself. As I worked in the kitchen, Grandpa would follow me around, telling me how he and his wife had managed their domestic affairs. Inevitably I would invite him to stay for dinner. Soon he was spending the nights too. He hung some of his paintings over the bed in the guest room. Slowly, very slowly, he sorted through his lifetime.

Every few nights Grandpa would return to his son's house. When he came back to ours, he would complain to me—his daughter-in-law was out working so the house was unkempt and dinners were late; the house was cold; his teenage grandchildren were uncivil. How different had been the home he had headed. Somehow, the men in his life remained faultless. They denied him nothing.

Grandpa spent more and more time with Lyle and me. In our seemingly big house I now had little privacy; more so, I had become the old man's companion and felt I was becoming his caretaker. I became resentful.

In the early spring blooming azaleas and dogwoods added color to our well-manicured suburban lawn. For some months Grandpa held onto his place in the house as if riding a bucking bronco while trying to remain the gentleman. Here he was, staying either in his son's uncomfortable house or in that of his grandson, who lived with his girlfriend of all things. I imagine disappointment came not from the particular circumstances but having arrived at the point of having to accept them. Reprieve came from another son who lived in California.

Over the next years Grandpa went from one son's home to another. Even though Lyle and I had gone our separate ways, I wrote Grandpa notes on cards with pretty pictures of flowers in vases.

One autumn I received in the mail Grandpa's wooden crumb duster, the one he and his wife had used for fifty years. Along with it came a note from a granddaughter telling me of his death and how much he had appreciated my letters over the years. I looked out the window—bare branches against a gray sky. There would be leaves in the spring.

THE DAY OF THE DRESS

When I got my first job out of college, in a county planning office, I didn't have much money to spend on a work wardrobe. My meager salary went to rent, utilities, transportation, and, oh yeah, food. Two other young women who were hired at the same time seemed to have more financial assets, and both dressed very well. One of them, Brett, and I became good work friends. Brett knew all about clothes and makeup. With her long blond hair, gold jewelry, well-made clothes, mascara and blue eyeshadow, she always turned the heads of our mostly male, mostly middle-age department. Brett could have taught me about makeup, but she always said that with my dark features I didn't need any, unlike her with her "disappearing" blond lashes and blue eyes.

We had some fun times together—driving around the county collecting streamwater samples, listening to blue grass music at a bar of West Virginia expats, escaping to the beach for a weekend, rafting the New River.

The thing that amazed me most about Brett was how charming she could be to everyone and how that gift illuminated her path wherever she went. Then, when we were alone, she would relish belittling everyone in the office and sharing her most intense dislikes. For me, who still struggles with keeping my emotions from expressing themselves clearly on my face, this was simultaneously fascinating and disturbing.

I cycled through my office clothes pretty much every week, recombining which blouse I wore with which dress pants or skirt. One day I finally took out a dress I had bought some years earlier but rarely wore, an Indian print cotton. I was modest, and the deep-V neckline of the dress was a bit too revealing. I got out a safety pin, closed the V up as high as I could, and went off to work.

Well, even with a safety pin the empire waist dress and V neck accentuated my bosom. Suddenly I had attention I had not known, nor desired, from my coworkers. Perhaps I had been dressing like a slouch. There was an abundance of good mornings, and suddenly my officemates had something to say to me. The day was surreal—I was the same person, but apparently the rest of my office didn't see me in the same light.

The next year I found another job with the county—in the water quality analysis lab. There I wore my scroungiest clothes under my white lab jacket because small splatters of acid were always a hazard.

Brett and I didn't stay in touch very long. Ours was a work friendship, and I had an intuitive inkling of the path she was leading me down. Anyway, the last time we talked she was rather preoccupied with luring away her mother's younger, good-looking boyfriend. Nothing in my closet could dress me up for that.

RISKY BUSINESS

TO BEE

To support myself during the summers of graduate school I worked as a research assistant to my advisor. He had made quite a name for himself by applying economic models to biological systems. The summer's question: to risk or not to risk.

We were studying the foraging behavior of bumblebees. We had enclosed a wild bumblebee colony in a cage (this small feat performed by a more courageous assistant, Jim) and presented the bees with artificial flowers.

Drop the notion of colorful silk inflorescences—or plastic ones for that matter. On top of a wood board painted green, we affixed blue and yellow plastic squares. Above our colorful square "flowers" we aligned a Plexiglas sheet that had small drilled depressions. We then pipetted precise quantities of honey solution into the indentations. In this way we could manipulate the honey rewards. One flower color was constant in its reward—that is, all the flowers received the same quantity of honey; the other color was variable—that is, some flowers had no honey whereas others received quantities far greater than that of our constant-reward flowers. By varying the constant reward and variable reward, we were to determine at what point the bees would prefer the variable flower color. They would risk receiving no honey because, on average, the variable flower yielded more honey—not unlike varying investment strategies. It was all very neat, in the cage.

Outside the cage was another story. The North Carolina summer days were long and hot. We became reckless, swatting yellow jackets that came to drink our honey solutions. Pulling ticks off became recreational sport. We soon discovered the bees had the sense to take a midday siesta. Being a distance from campus and home, we followed suit. Well, at least Jim and I did; our advisor soon realized that there was no real reason for him to stay most afternoons. Our summer's work was a success and resulted in a coauthored publication with some nice graphs demonstrating the bees' switching from risk-adverse to risk-prone behavior as the average reward of the variable flower increased.

I was taken with the rationality of foraging behavior, the underlying predictability given one could identify all the proximate parameters. I developed my own behavioral ecology research based on optimization theory.

The following summer we returned to the bee board, this time to ascertain whether individual bees demonstrated different switching behaviors—that is, whether individuals learned differently. Our advisor had learned that his intellectual powers were better spent elsewhere than at the bee board; that summer he pursued the Zen of pottery. We called him Master Buddha, and he often came at the end of the day to pick up the data. Jim had obtained funding to conduct his own bee experiments, so we called him Master Beta. Because I was still on my way to scientific research enlightenment, my appellation was Grasshopper. Bess, the undergraduate hired to work with me, needed no supplemental name. She was a force akin to entropy.

At the end of that summer came the end of our joint bumblebee era. Jim, the creative scientist he was, went on to pursue his doctorate with another mentor apparent. Bess, the passionate fool she was, decided to become a graduate student of Master Buddha. Risk adverse as he was, Master Buddha was convinced by us that the data set was insufficient to support his hypothesis and therefore did not publish that summer's work. And I, risk prone as I was, realized I was more interested in the scientists than the organisms, the abstractions than the data. I embarked on a future of highly unpredictable and variable rewards.

AS WITH ALL THINGS IN ~~LIFE~~ EDITING, BE CONSISTENT

I am a copy editor: I do more than correct English, less than rewrite paragraphs, usually.

My fare isn't novels or popular magazines but books of a scientific nature, often for professional audiences. I see my work as a collaboration with authors to make the best presentation of their work. To some, the language of science can seem dry, but I do appreciate the creative component of scientific endeavor.

One day I was writing a note to the typesetter regarding the book manuscript on which we were working. I wrote to her, "As with everything in life, be consistent." A quick keystroke edited my thought, but it was not as easily erased from my mind.

Be consistent—was that my guiding philosophy for life? As with many, my personality strengths have brought me to my work, and my work, in turn, has reinforced traits that are more desirable in moderation.

There are many skills I must call upon in copy editing. For example, I am required to remember numerous minute details at the same time I am considering broader-scale organization, content, and clarity. Having to keep all this in my head, I do miss details repeatedly and am required to backtrack—how was that name capitalized earlier in the book? Why is the abbreviation different here?

Perhaps the most important skills are having the willingness to recognize when I am uncertain and the patience to check the dictionary, a style guide, or, that gift, the internet. What amazes me about my work—well, about myself—is that during a project I know the book intimately, but once I have completed a project I barely can remember the title.

I have learned a lot about writing from editing. Editing has taught me about precision and clarity of thought and organization. Poor writing may obscure clear thought, and good writing can obscure the lack of thought—but not for long.

With each job I learn something about the profession to which I have arrived haphazardly. For example, although within-manuscript consistency is paramount, it is important to understand the rules and objectives well enough to know when it is appropriate to deviate. After all, clarity for the reader should hold sway.

Likewise in life I am attacking my tendency toward consistency, although I think some old friends treasure me for it.

Correctness, consistency, clarity—there is one *C*-word, however, that led me away from doing science, for I could not express it there; neither is it satisfied in editing. That word is creativity. It is the creative component of the process that makes the endeavor worth doing. I have to shake this consistency thing. Detail is in the art, but art is not in the details.

FIVE PAGES

It was in the local library—a grand building at the corner of Bushwick and DeKalb Avenues in Brooklyn—when the desire crystallized. I was ten, give or take a year, and I must have been reading a wonderful book. I declared to myself I wanted to be a writer: I too wanted to create the wonderful, intimate world that I found in books.

This desire stayed in the back of my mind as other career choices were weighed—ballerina, astronaut, spy—but I never saw any other career as mutually exclusive. Even when I went to college I still had a sense that I could—would—write in addition to whatever course of study I pursued. But along the way, as I delved deeper into science, the idea of me as writer became buried—that is, until the ripe age of twenty-five when an old boyfriend reminded me of what I wanted to be at sixteen.

Writing became a part of my life, although it was still pursued in conjunction with something else. I started a novel while still a graduate student in ecology and continued to work on it while employed as a research technician. Once I had my first child I switched to short personal narratives, such as this one. There were great lapses in writing—more so once I had my second child. Often there was no writing, for there was no time or energy between kids and trying to maintain a "day job."

Then I reached a point at which enough mental space was freed that I could return to "what I really want to be." I had a finished novel, a few dozen essays, and a novel in progress. I set to work on learning how to get my work published and soon realized, as those before me, that this part of the job would be as hard as—no, harder than—the writing.

I researched, submitted, and had my work rejected. I researched some more, submitted some more, and had my work rejected some more. Then I had some small successes, albeit rather small. Two agents agreed to look at my first novel and quite kindly told me it was not right for them. One offered to look at my work in progress when it was completed: "Send me the first five pages."

The first five pages! More than the paragraph of a query letter, less than one would hope for given the daunting undertaking of creating a novel. I did not fault the agent and know now this is a standard and generous offer—apparently, publishers may give no more than a line.

I sat for the next few days, trying to work on my second novel, wondering how I could rearrange the beginning I had written so that I could "grab" the reader. In reality, an unknown writer may have at most a paragraph to do so. Still, I can't help but think of all the books I have read and loved that required an investment of more than five pages. One of those books, perhaps the very book that set me on the path that day at the library, was *Knee Deep in Thunder* by Sheila Moon. In it, a young girl enters a world of insects and is drafted into a challenging quest; in the journey she affirms herself. Admittedly the book sounds suspiciously like my first novel, albeit any such similarities were not intentional.

I eventually was able to calm myself and return to work on my book, developing my characters and developing my story. The novel is complete, sitting in a virtual drawer. It stays there between bouts of submissions and rejections, between believing in myself and doubting myself. I am still on that challenging journey.

THE TREE OF LIFE

THE TREE OF LIFE

The slide showed a dirt road enveloped in a misty shroud. At the side of the road a beautiful red flower with a yellow lip stood out against the wet green blades of grass. Pebbles glistened. "What is it?" I asked Ryan. "A weed," he replied.

I am not very good at remembering the names of plants and animals, but many of my friends take pride in their familiarity with the biota of home and beyond. There is a branch of biology involved in the naming and identification of organisms, taxonomy; implicit to this discipline is the field of systematics, the classification of organisms. Biological classification is hierarchical—species are grouped into genera, which, in turn, are grouped into families, and so on. Theoretically, at the end of the search for the natural order is the one tree of life.

In the 1980s I worked in a systematics lab for six years as a technician. I did not become as well versed in the field as did the graduate students around me, but I did acquire a basic vocabulary. The words are long and their meanings complex, but a few words provide a basic orientation. Plesiomorphies are characters, or qualities, that species inherit from their primitive ancestors. Synapomorphies are new, unique characters that two or more species share and that establish their relatedness.

Biologists come to their disciplines with different motivations, and, as most of us are influenced by the work we do, they take from their disciplines perceptions about the world. Being an organized type, I found the promise of a natural order alluring. However, systematics is not only about existing patterns but about how they came to be—in other words, historical lineages.

Ryan told me excitely one day that he had learned that his mother's family had been in the United States since the seventeenth century and had been an original Maryland family, receiving extensive land grants. His family could trace its roots to some great Norman ruler. "Of course, every family has its distribution of kings and scoundrels," he quipped. "Your name is probably polyphyletic"—a term for species having similar characters but derived from different lineages. "Names that refer to trades usually are." We returned to our work, each pursuing his piece of the tree—Ryan writing his tome on a group of beetles, I measuring the length of moth legs.

Gracile dendritic arms merge to form a heavier limb, which, in turn, joins with other branches to form a stout bough, and so on—until the trunk of the tree of life finds root in Mother Earth. Indeed, there may be one tree of life. From it we can learn about evolution and relatedness; from it we can learn about chance and circumstance. New buds, new limbs, old limbs, full limbs, sparse limbs, dead limbs—but not better limbs.

I am a weed that grew in Brooklyn. I delight in our plesiomorphies.

MOTH GENITALIA I.

People give me gifts with insect motifs. Just because I once worked with insects doesn't mean I identify with them. Never mind that I wrote a novel in which the main character, somewhat reminiscent of myself, is a mayfly.

As a graduate student I studied mayflies and other stream-dwelling insects. After I earned my Master's degree I went to work as a research assistant in moth systematics. Systematics is the study of how groups of organisms are related. In practice we searched for similarities and differences among species of a few genera of moths in order to reconstruct their lineage.

I knew little of moths when I started my employment, but they soon became the conduit for important life experiences. My first project in the lab was one for which I had to kill just-hatched caterpillars from several female moths to determine which caterpillars were genetically identical—that is, which were produced asexually. This work demanded that I face a complicated moral issue: did individuals of a clone share one soul or did each have her own soul? How many deaths would be counted against me?

Another task early in my apprenticeship was to remove and clean the legs of dried moth specimens. The procedure involved dissolving the soft tissue from inside the leg and then brushing—with a fine camel hair brush—the scales from the outside of the leg. I then compared the legs of different species. Hour upon hour of looking at moth legs paid off. I discovered a certain turn in the tarsal claw that was key to distinguishing between two closely related groups of moths. What the power of observation will do! I became a coauthor.

Moths became emblazoned upon my psyche. I dreamt of moth legs stuck between my teeth. In dreams I worked through the night, struggling to see the relationships among species and genera, straining to find the character that would make all the pieces fit in a crystal-clear "family" tree. I was searching for the truth that hid in the data, apparent yet obscured—until one could find the right question.

When I wondered what I was doing with my life I would reflect that Vladimir Nabokov also dallied with the Lepidoptera.

But I was not a genuine lepidopterist, taken by the turn of a velvet wing. I just worked with moths. As I graduated from legs to wings to genitalia, I became a skilled technician to an esoteric pursuit. My eyes and hands focused on chitinous structures that held keys of identity and affinity. My struggle was to maintain my peripheral vision.

The technician often is an invisible being in the hierarchy of academia and like institutions. In the academic hierarchy everyone is given a place, and that place qualifies the strength of one's voice. Amidst those who have achieved an often hard-won professional status and graduate students aspiring for the same, someone who is not on a like path must somehow be incapable of the rigors. This sentiment is not universal, nor is the contribution of a good technician always overlooked, but the general sentiment can be quite oppressive to a technician's ego. As time went on, I learned little more about moths but had the lesson about my place repeated too often.

Fortunately, the investigators lost their grant, and I lost my job.

The fine features of a moth can amaze anyone who has the interest to take a close look. I found pleasure in brushing away scales to reveal the structure beneath. In academia I looked for affinities while exploring my identity. I searched for the character that would make all the pieces fit.

MOTH GENITALIA II.

I had a friend, Lillian, who seemed as delicate as the butterflies she studied. Some beings keep their secrets well hidden.

Lillian and I both studied leps— Lepidoptera—she, butterflies, and I, moths. Through the microscope we examined heads, wings, legs, and trunks, looking for scales and spines that might distinguish one species from another. We dissected lep genitalia, looking for secrets of species identity. First we would cut off the abdomen with sharp, thin forceps; then we would soak it in a solution to dissolve the body tissue; and finally, we would clean it with our forceps, fine brushes, and hypodermic needles filled with water until we obtained aesthetically pleasing chitinized structures in their bared glory.

Many of our specimens had been dead for some time—animals stored respectfully in museum drawers after having been collected by entomologists of days gone by. Some specimens had been collected much more recently, and the tissue in their bodies took longer to dissolve. I preferred that my animals came to me long dead.

In general, female Lepidoptera have the less interesting reproductive structures—or the more subtle. It is the males who have the flashy gadgets. There is a theory that suggests that some species ensure they don't mate with closely related species by means of the males and females possessing close-fitting reproductive parts; the theory is referred to as the lock-and-key theory of reproductive isolation. At one time, Lillian was terminating butterfly copulations and dissecting the mating pair to examine just how the pair's structures interlocked. Lillian found the esoteric world she had chosen to explore fascinating.

Lillian was a rare specimen herself—a black woman in a traditionally white male field. Lillian softly crossed barriers that had tended to isolate, perhaps in search of a world that would insulate. She delved into the world of butterfly form, classification, and evolution; there was Zen in the dissecting, art in the illustrating, and creativity in the intellectual pursuit. And from it all, Lillian hoped to reconstruct what had been in order to explain what is; the past would elucidate the intricacies of the present. The evidence was in chitinized structures, in fragments of DNA.

But Lillian was not happy with the intricacies of her present. Perhaps she did not find her place, her relationship. Perhaps the grace of forms left her wanting for perfection. Lillian, quiet and soft spoken, curious and determined, ended her life.

Those of us she left behind sorted through the interactions and conversations we had and didn't have with her, trying to reconstruct the history, searching for some truth, some understanding, looking for a story that satisfied our needs.

Once a genitalia dissection was completed, we would place what remained of the specimen—its head, thorax, and wings—back in its box and then back in its drawer. So much life is lost in the pursuit.

A LITTLE PIECE OF MY HEART

BLUEBIRDS, BLUEBELLS, AND LOVE

I met Stephen two days after his wife and their unborn child had died. Jennifer, who would have become my sister-in-law, was killed by a careless driver. Having barely met my boyfriend's family, I arrived to share their worst moment.

Stephen and my friendship came to define the word bittersweet to me. My boyfriend, Jim, had spent a lot of time with his sister and Stephen in the past, and now Stephen spent time with us. There were cold days in the Shenandoah Valley looking for bluebirds and warm days along the

Shenandoah River looking for bluebells; there were floats on the river and spills into the river; there were trips to the Eastern Shore and wet, smelly trips home with Stephen's two cocker spaniels; there were days of dancing at folk-life festivals and evenings of Stephen playing the fiddle; and then there were those long, sparse phone conversations when Stephen wanted— needed—company, but there was so little to say.

Even in his sadness, Stephen kept his sense of humor. Seeing my snobbish urban streak, he invited me to see a *film* with an appropriate foreign-sounding title. He quickly ushered me into the theater, and it took me a few minutes to realize that I wasn't watching haute-culture passion but instead a porn flick. One of my fondest memories is of making Stephen laugh. I was wearing my University of New Hampshire t-shirt. "What does U-N-H stand for?" he asked, and I grunted, "unh."

But Stephen's sadness overwhelmed him. Jennifer had made his life work, and without her he began to unravel. He pushed us away. He no longer called or wrote. He didn't respond to my letters. A few years went by in this state of affairs.

I continued to send him notes periodically. In one I enclosed a self-addressed envelope and response sheet on which he could construct a letter out of options I had given him. He returned the note with a message, and I was optimistic. We received news from Jim's mother that Stephen had been in touch with her and was taking positive steps— returning to school, folk dancing again, dating.

Not long after that there was a phone call. While riding home on his bicycle, Stephen had been struck by a car—a drunk driver. He was in a coma.

Going to see Stephen was painful. Any little movement gave one hope, even though the movements were likely meaningless. Six months later, Stephen died.

For a long time in my dreams I continued to include Stephen in family gatherings. Some years later, when I was pregnant, I dreamt of Jim's family being at the beach, a place where they like to gather. Stephen was there, and I was so happy to see him. I knew this was my opportunity—I went to him and silently placed his hand on my stomach.

I think of Stephen whenever I think of bluebirds, bluebells, or love.

TAKE ANOTHER LITTLE PIECE OF MY HEART

Susan and I never were the closest of friends. Our paths crossed at a university—Jim and her husband became friends, and we all ended up spending time together.

Susan and Doug were a slightly older, conservative couple, and Doug's staid manner never deviated from this assessment. Although Susan had been raised in a conventional, religious (Christian) household, there was a wild streak in her, due to, in part, her unbridled, unabashed openness. For one thing, she didn't hesitate to talk about sex: mixed- and not-mixed-company conversations with her would turn me red.

What Susan and I shared was a kind of faith in honesty: if one always strived to be honest with others, one must be honest with oneself, and this honesty would allow one both internal harmony and connection to the world beyond self.

Even then, I explored honesty and "truth" through writing. I am more skeptical of the motivations for my writing now. Knowledge is imperfect; memories are revisions. At times what I write is, in part, an effort to make experiences more palatable.

I do have a crystal-clear memory of Susan's and my finest moment, though. At a party, without a care for onlookers, sweating profusely, we unabashedly ground to Janis Joplin: "Come on, come on, come on, come on and take it! Take another little piece of my heart now, baby . . ." It was a completely sensual experience.

Circumstance brought us all—Susan and Doug, myself and Jim—to a new location together. Instead of the move fortifying our relationship, Susan and I drifted apart. At the time I was uncertain about what I was doing with my life whereas Susan, after much determined effort, had borne her first child and was focused on being a mother. We still spent time together, but our lives were diverging.

As is typical in academia, a few years later Susan and Doug moved again, and Susan and I drifted further apart. We wrote once or twice a year and kept abreast of the major developments in one another's lives.

Then in one letter, after news of her two children and Doug, as if an afterthought, Susan wrote that she had undergone a mastectomy. A few years later she wrote that the cancer had metastasized and was in her spine. I procrastinated but eventually called her; then I procrastinated longer—too long. At the age of thirty-nine Susan died, leaving behind Doug and their two children, eight and eleven.

This is the truth Susan: I didn't call because I didn't know how to talk to a dying friend.

Break another little bit of my heart.

WILL YOU COME TO ARKANSAS?

One doesn't know where one will end up living. When Jim was being considered for a position in Arkansas, I asked my friend, Lillian, "Will you visit me in Arkansas?" Head down, she smiled her demure tee-hee smile and simply said, "No."

It is sometimes within life's transitory experiences that one forms deep and lasting friendships. With whom one remains in contact sorts itself out in time: there are those friendships that transcend time and circumstance, those conversations that can be resumed whenever friends meet again, and those friends who are just good about calling, writing, or visiting. Yet even if one stays in touch with those who leave or those one has left, the unique shared context of time and place is forever gone.

Lillian had managed almost to complete her doctorate without ever moving more than thirty miles from home, and there were signs she didn't plan on moving much farther upon its completion. Her preferred milieu was Washington, D.C.

When I first met Lillian in an entomology lab, my thought was to engage her with conversation of research and bugs. I got little from the soft-spoken, quiet woman. Then one day I said something about my father and his lady friend and found an inroad: Lillian loved to hear and tell about family—the more outrageous the story, the better. I became willing to tell anything, make any kind of fool of myself, to see Lillian laugh and smile. Whence this devotion? Perhaps the original challenge of making her smile continued to inspire me. But more so, I quickly recognized that behind her reserved exterior was an incredibly open mind—I could tell her *anything* and have her rapt attention, yet she seemed to apply no preconceived notion to me or what I said. Our conversations pursued nuances that likely would have bored others. Lillian's openness and focus served her in her intellectual life as well: she could absorb herself in the pursuit of understanding some arcane phenomenon or theory. Her problem was, at times, not knowing when to surface before becoming mired.

Luckily Jim didn't get the job in Arkansas— the rain and mosquitoes would have done me in. Even so, I saw less and less of Lillian. We no longer worked in the same lab. She was busy pursuing her doctorate; I was working to establish myself as an editor. She had separated from her husband of many years and was dating other men; I had just had a baby. We relished one another's company when together, but there were long lapses between our visits, lapses that became longer and more frequent. Lillian became unavailable.

One May morning, a few days after a party at which I had seen Lillian for the first time in over a month, Lillian was dead. At first we thought her death was somehow related to her diabetes. Within a few weeks we learned she had taken cyanide, the poison entomologists use for their insects. Quite discretely, and quite hidden, Lillian had suffered from depression.

Not soon after Lillian's death, Jim was offered a job in Texas, and we decided to take it. We had been in Maryland a long time and were leaving many good friends. I had thought Lillian would be the one who always remained there—instead she was the one who made it time to leave.

I dreamt of Lillian often. In one dream I met her in a field. The sun was bright, and she wouldn't look up or talk to me. I followed her into an old barn, where she made her way toward a dark stall. She opened a door and paused before an earthen stairway into the ground. She looked at me, as if asking if I would go with her. In the raucous voice I often used to bring a smile to her face, I simply said, "No."

WHERE TO WEAR MY STAR OF DAVID

A CONFUSED CHILD

On an airplane flight some years ago, I had one of those candid conversations one has at times with a stranger. I was reading *The Fellowship of the Rings*, and our conversation began there, went on to good and evil, and then turned to religion. The stranger was a Jesuit, and he was deeply interested in Judaism and assumed I had a much greater understanding of my own religion than I did or do. At one point he asked me what I found to be the most difficult aspect of

Judaism. I doubt I gave him the type of answer he expected. I said, "As I child I used to wonder what the Jews had done to make so many others hate them."

I was a child of a generation to whom the Holocaust was real and recent. I also was a child growing up in the Bushwick section of Brooklyn in the 1960s, which made me a double minority— White and Jewish. It was an odd position to be in among my classmates, who were mostly Black and Puerto Rican. The other Jews in their world were teachers and shop owners. At times my Jewishness earned me unwanted favoritism from teachers—making life among my peers a bit difficult—but for the most part my peers saw me as separate from the world of Jewish adults, whom they perceived as having all the wealth and power. I remember clearly a day when a classmate, upon seeing President Johnson on the TV screen, said something—not very nice—about him being a Jew. I knew little about the larger world, but I knew enough to respond, "*They* wouldn't let a Jew be president."

I was pretty confused as a child about what it meant to be Jewish, even though my parents started sending me, with my siblings, to the local *shul* when I was nine. I think much of this confusion wasn't any different from a child's general confusion about the world—negotiating its unknown rules and complicated fabric. Judaism just added an extra layer, particularly because it was different from so much of the world I saw around me that had to do with Christmas, Easter, and Jesus. I remember once, at a very young age, I volunteered to sing a Jewish Christmas song in class. *Oy gevalt!* Was I mixed up!

I also attributed various family values to Judaism. At school fights among girls—and between the sexes—were not that uncommon. When some of my more pugnacious classmates would try to goad me into a fight, I would declare it was against my religion. After all, to my mind, this must have accounted for how the Holocaust occurred. I don't recall how I reconciled this view with the Six Day War.

My family moved just before I entered middle school, and there I found myself in class with many other Jews, and that itself proved to be a perplexing experience—the unwritten rules were quite different. On through high school, college, work, and living in multiple states—at times I encountered nuanced, and not so nuanced, anti-Semitism. Through most of that time, though, being Jewish was not part of my self-identity; I found it largely irrelevant to my life except when others didn't. When I moved to Texas, though, I was motivated to learn more about Judaism because I was raising my children in an environment in which religion, that is, Christianity, permeated everyday life, including the public school system. For the most part, people I have met in Texas have been curious albeit ignorant about Judaism. Admittedly, I have asserted my Jewishness here on a one-person mission to promote awareness of diversity.

In ways there is not much distance between who I am today and that young child, confused as to why a group she belongs to by birth is hated by people she does not know and who do not know her. This is the face of prejudice, though, and I cannot help but think of the children who continue to experience it each day.

THE LAST BAR MITZVAH

Sometimes people whom I barely knew, people long dead, come to my mind. Their faces are indistinct, but I remember a yearning they expressed that, as a child, I was too young to understand.

These memories come upon hearing songs—the melodies familiar, the words foreign—songs in Hebrew, sung for generations of which we each belong to only one.

I learned these songs as a child in my *shul.* It was home to a remnant Jewish community in Bushwick. My siblings and I, four of us, typically constituted half the Sunday school class. Our parents, children of immigrants who wanted their children to be Americanized, received no formal Jewish education. Now living in a multi-ethnic but largely Christian community, my parents wanted their own children to know something of what it meant to be Jewish.

The *shul* was a three-story, semi-attached row house. On the ground floor were the rabbi's office and a modest sanctuary. Most singing, however, occurred either in the upstairs Sunday school classroom or in the basement, where there was a large social hall. I remember singing the words I didn't understand—which mattered little if I liked the melody—in this large room full of old people. Now I know the sense of yearning I remember was embedded in the minor key of those melodies.

During my childhood, Jews were mostly older people, and most of them seemed to be very old people. They had remained in our revolving immigrant neighborhood through its subsequent transformations, perhaps because they had already experienced leaving their homes in Europe. The women would come, shrunken by age, small fur stoles draped about their shoulders; their husbands wore black wool coats. We would eat *hamantaschen* together and drink diluted Manischewitz.

The pinnacle of my family's life at the *shul* was my brother's *bar mitzvah.* It was quite an affair for my parents to host—my aunt and uncle came all the way from Florida. The entire congregation was invited, and it seemed they were filled with as much excitement as my family. We girls, three of us, all got new dresses—a rarity. My parents hired caterers for the reception, and my grandfather, acting as bartender, got drunk. My brother received enough money in gifts to buy a piano.

Soon after the *bar mitzvah* my family moved, and the *shul* closed.

When I hear a song from this past, I remember those now-faded congregants. My brother's *bar mitzvah* was not his own or his family's but that of a community passing, a neighborhood *shul* that had come to the end of its life.

The melody comes back, sometimes the words, and I sing the song that has been sung for generations. The dead live again, and I add my voice to the history.

WHERE TO WEAR MY STAR OF DAVID

At a luncheon in my honor when I left my first real job at the ripe old age of twenty-two, I was presented with a Star of David pendant. My face showed my discomfort. "Don't you like it?" asked Luanne, my middle-age, Baptist officemate who had selected the gift. "You never wear one . . . I thought you needed one." Ungraciously I responded, "I *choose* not to wear one." I still regret the brusqueness of my reply, but I still find religion a private thing.

In the mid-1990s, I moved to a small, Christian town in Texas—me, an urban, agnostic Jew. In the first few weeks I was there several of my new acquaintances asked, "What church will you be attending?" With my convenient hex to ward off such invasions, I answered, "I'm Jewish." "Oh," came the polite response. Thankfully, the door to that topic was closed. But it wasn't.

You see, I brought with me my young son, who would grow up in this town. Whereas my husband was leery, to put it mildly, of religious training, I was worried what would happen if we allowed a religious vacuum. Hence, I concluded my son would become more Jewish here than he might have elsewhere. But what should I teach him? If we were in a Jewish community, he could have assimilated his heritage. Instead, I had to brush up on my Judaism.

Between the ages of nine and eleven I was sent to Hebrew class once a week with my brother and, at most, three other students. One day a young boy from a bohemian family was arguing heatedly with the rabbi, I don't recall over what. I remember the boy's final words, which stung the rabbi: "I don't even believe in God." It was the first time it occurred to me that any of this—Hebrew school, Sunday school, being Jewish—had anything to do with believing in God. And if it were not for the rabbi's strong reaction, I probably would have continued in my ignorance. That day I asked myself if I believed in God, and I didn't really know. I leaned toward yes only because I didn't want to disappoint a figure of authority, the rabbi, even if I didn't like him.

There are things I am comfortable with in the Jewish religion—that the "clergy" are not intermediaries between the lay and God; that every person is expected to assume the obligations of being a responsible member of society; and that knowledge and learning are requisites to piety.

My agnosticism is not a lack of faith in humankind and our capacity for good, it is not an abdication of moral and responsible behavior, and it is not an absence of a sense of purpose. These were the tenets I hoped to teach my son—these and a belief in the sanctity of all living things. What would fall under the guise of Judaism I did not know. Judaism would foremost be his cultural heritage, as it has been mine. To the religious Jew, I am probably the worst variety.

A friend who converted to Judaism some years ago commented that Judaism accommodates doubtful brethren. With this thought, I brought my son to a service in a nearby city. "*Sh'ma yisrael Adonai Eloheinu Adonai ehad.*" This familiar, ancient chant seemed to welcome me to my place among an ancient people. I felt a sorely missed sense of belonging, even if transient, in my strange, new land.

I wear no hexagram on my chest, but I carry my beliefs in my heart. For me, after all, religion is a private thing.

MIDLIFE MEANDERS

THE GRAND CANYON

On the eve of my fortieth birthday I visited the Grand Canyon for the first time. I had felt older since the birth of my first son, no longer connected to a younger self. I suspected I was gearing up for my midlife crisis and that it probably would be typical and not much different from my biannual crisis regarding what I was doing with my life.

Jim, our son, and I made this side trip on a 1,700-mile winding course from Texas to California. A steady snow fell on the road out of Flagstaff, and I nervously wondered whether we should turn back. We forged on, the snow abated, and we stopped at the first point at which we could catch a glimpse of the canyon. With car- and busloads of other visitors we stepped out on windswept Mather Point. We waited our turn for an unobstructed view. Yes, the canyon was as big and deep and spectacular as we had imagined. I took photos.

On the first night of our trip west, we had camped at Caprock Canyons in the panhandle of Texas. We spent the morning there, walking one of the trails. Dramatic cliffs of red shales, sandstones, siltstones, and mudstones laced with white gypsum surrounded us, holding stories 250 million years old. Vegetation was sparse. We were the only visitors in the park that cold morning, and as I walked through one windy, dark pass, I felt a thrill: the unknown lying in wait beyond. I stopped on the other side of the pass; the trail beckoned me on, but it was time to turn back.

We travel in life. I do not believe we have predetermined paths, but I do believe we are products of histories that date well before our birth. Still, where one's path leads is unpredictable.

My path has been a meandering one, and on that trip I found myself reflecting on things that as a younger woman I had expected to do and now realized I might never attain. At various junctures I made choices of direction from among what appeared to be my options; now I wondered if my perception of those options had been limited.

But my meandering has been a learning process. In my travels I have lost and found myself again and again. Each finding is a rebirth.

On the eve of my fortieth, leaving the Grand Canyon after the most superficial of visits, I laughed at my "we were here" photos. Living occurs in the depth of the experience: as a mother, experiencing a child's utter dependency; as an individual, trying to find the mental space to maintain myself amid my responsibilities; and as a maturing adult, learning what to accept and when to move on.

CATHARSES #43 AND #45

#43: Dragonflies

I went home the summer of my forty-third year with my husband and two boys for an extended stay. Home is East. I brought a lot of baggage with me.

Finding a happy medium between visiting friends and family and relaxing was hard. I desperately wanted to fill up on the richness and depth of old friendships, but that was difficult with a heathen of a two-year-old.

Some visits were better than others, and at times I was surprised at my success at having substantive conversations. But still, I was not sated, and as the discord grew between my hunger and the sustenance, I found myself trying to assess what it meant to be middle-aged. A lot of it seemed to be about finding a comfortable compromise between youthful expectations and dwindling possibilities, desires and realities, individual and family needs.

I became so weary by the end of the trip. There were no breaks from being a mom. My desire for some insightful morsel grew: I awaited a catharsis. Maybe one did come—so fleeting, I almost missed it.

My two-year-old was napping, and my mother-in-law was watching him. I took my seven-year-old and his friend to the river. The boys ran off to explore the shallow riffles. I entered the river and walked upstream to the pooled waters. It was a quiet day. I sank to just below my lower lip. The surface was murky with a solid greenish-brown sheen. I perceived the current only by the small flecks of pollen and leaves that drifted past me. Damselflies chased one another across the surface—males chasing males, males chasing females, males chasing mating pairs. Males and females in copula floated on fallen leaves. Their needs, their destinies, were intense and unambiguous. I stood up. I had found a brief moment of peace in a timeless world larger than my own.

#45: The Yellow Balloon

For much of my adult life, my parents and in-laws lived halfway across the country. Whether we visited for weeks or months, we always reached the point at which we took our leave, and with years it became harder to say goodbye. Knowing much time would pass before our next visit, knowing we lived our daily lives without extended family, I began to become overwhelmed with a sense that one of these partings would be a final goodbye, that our time together was finite.

I have lived away from family since the age of seventeen, and several major moves have taken me away from good friends made along the way. I have had the foresight to retain valuable connections in a lifetime filled with translocations. From a very young age I sensed that the here and now would change with time— a sense that the present would be lost forever. Perhaps this is why I record—in my writing and my voluminous photo collection. I try to capture what is because I am aware of its fleeting nature.

The summer I was forty-five my mother was so excited that her four children would be in town at the same time, with three of her four grandchildren, that she planned a big shindig on Father's Day. She bought food and drink and balloons. She invited relatives and old family friends—several people I hadn't seen for fifteen years or more. It was a crowded, noisy affair, and by hour three, my four-year-old was totally spent. I found him clinging to a big yellow balloon, one of the only ones that had not yet popped. He looked despondent.

"What's wrong?" I asked, scooping him up.

"I'm sad because I like my balloon so much, and I know it's going to pop."

Whenever the melancholy of saying goodbye overwhelms me, I think of that yellow balloon. I must enjoy what I love while it is here and not dwell on its ephemeral nature.

BOLUS #48

Whether it was post-new-house-construction exhaustion or too many PTA meetings, I spent the spring of my forty-eighth year in an unfocused, unmotivated, and overwhelmed state. As always, I looked toward the summer visit home to rejuvenate me, but as time passed I became even more depleted.

That year our plans and circumstances led us to delay the New York City segment of our trip to the end of our eastern sojourn. My eighty-one-year-old father was being denied his dignity in old age as his body—but not his mind—shut down and robbed him of his independence. Meanwhile, my eighty-year-old mother was undergoing a medication-induced renaissance that was somewhat akin to adolescence.

Jim and I arrived with our two boys and bags and tried to spread around the trauma we inflicted. My family wanted us to visit, but the reality of two young boys in apartment space— four extra people to move around—lost its luster quickly.

First we stayed with my sister. She was busy with a job to which she was devoted. At home was her companion who had a disabling stroke in his mid-forties. His ability to communicate limited, he still dominated the living space and my sister's attentions.

My brother had more space to offer. Having just broken off his relationship, he had no companion to accommodate. But being somewhere between the highs and lows of his moods, he was tense, agitated.

My mother, in her thin, rejuvenate form, spent a day with us. She was so happy to see her grandchildren, and I assumed we would see her more. But her new male friend called her. He wanted her to come and help him pack for a move. We did not see her again.

If I had gone to New York City to see anyone, it was my father who cannot travel. He was not in a good state and tried to share with me how he felt. He was sorry he could not be part of the family get-togethers. He was sorry he could not interact more with our boys. He told me he felt deserted by his body—he couldn't do the very few things that were left to him before his most recent hospitalization. I would never ask, but I thought perhaps he also felt deserted a second time around by my mother. She had been visiting him regularly those last few years; since this new man came into her life, she only called.

I realized how my mother, whose behavior was reminiscent of her behavior when she left the family, had taken us all back more than thirty years. As I did then, I left to save myself. Thank goodness my younger sister wasn't in New York City for another round.

My kids used to watch a very silly movie, "Kung Pao Enter the Fist." At one point the main character buys a large bag of nuts, and the vendor loudly declares, "That's a lot of nuts!" My sons found this hilarious. My visit to New York City that summer was stressful; as soon as I left I felt better. As we drove away I couldn't help saying to myself, "That's a lot of nuts!", which made me realize I was in relatively good shape. It was time to pull myself together and get on with life.

LIVING ON THE BACKBONE

CHICKEN LOVE

"Those are some plump-looking hens you have for this country," commented a new visitor to our home. "Lots of table scraps from the kids," Jim responded, opening the screen door. "We've already lost some," my voice trailed from the kitchen.

Growing up I never imagined that chickens were in my future. I was on my third cohort.

Shortly after we moved to our new home, one mile down a gravel road in Central Texas, Jim decided to pursue a childhood pleasure—raising chickens. One day he came home with five

Ameraucana chicks. We put the chicks in our cracked bathtub, and Jim went to work on a deluxe coop with four arched doorways, a nice roost pole, and a shingled roof.

Soon the chicks were hens and were laying exquisite copper-flecked green eggs. Now I was a chicken enthusiast. I had never known the difference between the richness of a fresh egg and a puny store-bought one. Along with the appeal of self-sufficiency, I liked turning table scraps into new food. However, the wildlife that we enjoyed around our home proved to be less than advantageous to chickens. The first two cohorts weren't with us very long. We decided to take a hiatus from raising chickens.

Then one day my two sons and I stopped at the feed store, and lo and behold there was a cattle tank full of chicks. The boys picked up almost every one, and when it was time to leave I was pulling both boys, crying, from the store. I headed straight for Jim's office, the instigator of this chicken affair, and soon we were all back at the feed store. I picked a tiny red chick and promptly named her "The Little Red Hen" after the fictional character with whom I often identified. The guys picked three Ameraucanas, and then my younger son, Leland, insisted on one more—a black chick, which he named "Booboo."

We constructed a fenced yard around the coop to give the chickens more space on days that our otherwise free-ranging chickens should be kept locked up—for instance, if an unleashed dog had been sighted. Little Red, and she was diminutive, was the first to lay an egg—a petite brown one. She and Booboo, who grew to be enormous and laid large brown eggs, became our most prolific layers. The three Ameraucanas, whom the boys aptly named Fluffy, Wildy, and Fasty, consistently were naughty girls who built clandestine nests in the woods.

For a while we had three roosters, rescued by Jim from a coworker. We quickly learned that three roosters were far too many for five hens. They hounded the hens relentlessly. Leland reported that the roosters kept "picking the fleas off Fluffy." Little Red was losing feathers! We gave away two of the roosters, and before long the lone rooster wandered off and was gone.

Then came a very sad day—the day Leland discovered a pile of Little Red's feathers. We collected them in a shoebox and buried them alongside our other dear, departed pets for whom my sons had grieved.

More than anything, loose dogs remained the greatest threat to our chickens. We saved them repeatedly from the jaws of neighbors' pets. One day, home alone, I answered the chickens' alarm call to find a beagle mix snapping after them. I lost my head and screamed, "Get out of here! I'll kill you! I'll kill you if you come back!" I wonder what my neighbors thought. I wonder what my New York City mother would say.

Booboo eventually had gray in her tail feathers and didn't lay many eggs. The Ameraucanas built a nest at the base of a juniper tree near the house. The pecking order, which my older son, Silas, monitored, changed over time.

One day long after Little Red had died, I picked up Leland from daycare. His teacher told me he had been sobbing. "He was on his mat looking up at his poster"—the poster, "My Family," included a picture of my guys holding Little Red and her first egg. "He broke out in tears, and when I asked him what was wrong, he said, 'I miss Little Red.' He cried for a long time."

From deep love flows deep grief.

THE ONE THAT GOT AWAY

Blanco was the chicken that started the last cycle, the cycle that begins with joy and inevitably leads to resigned sadness. The length of each cycle is highly variable, but each ends by snake, hawk, or quadruped.

Blanco arrived still in egg. A neighbor called asking us to take in the chicks of a pathological hen that was pecking her babies to death. Blanco arrived with one sibling, already pecked above the eye. When Blanco's egg hadn't hatched by the end of the day, Silas carefully peeled her out of her shell.

For days Silas and Leland cuddled the chicks, trying to keep Blanco's sibling from scratching its sore. But there was no way to protect the chick from itself, and its screams were painful to all of us. After a few days, Jim ended the chick's life. I've been called to this duty too—compassionate killing. It is not a facile chore.

Because chickens are social animals, we soon bought three Ameraucana chicks to keep Blanco company. Silas and Leland gave them Spanish—

and, regardless of sex, masculine—names too: Loco for the chick that pecked the others' toes; Stupido for the chick that was not as precocious as its cohort and turned out to be a rooster; and Diego because it was fun to pronounce as if a character in a spaghetti western.

Blanco, a bantam, grew quickly and soon outsized the purchased chicks. That brief tenure as largest chick earned her an unwonted place in the pecking order. For as the Ameraucanas grew to their much larger adult size, Blanco never grew much larger than a mourning dove. But her size belied her fierceness and independence. She intimidated the other two hens and spent most of her time with the rooster. She often wandered off on her own, and she foraged among the wild turkeys as well as among the various species of doves that stopped in the yard for seed and water.

We had a happy flock. Leland was the chicken whisperer. He talked to them, they answered. If he walked outside, they came. They followed him everywhere, and even the ornery rooster allowed himself to be carried and stroked. But then the attrition started—one evening we returned home just past dusk and Diego was gone. Leland shed his tears, hugged the remaining chickens, and added the loss to the many he had suffered.

It became clear quite early that Blanco was determined to become a mother—perhaps to prove that her mother's illness was not hereditary. We were uncertain as to whether her eggs were even fertile—she literally could back out of Stupido's attempted couplings. But one winter she sat on her nest of tiny white eggs peppered with the much larger green eggs of Loco. She sat, and when it seemed the eggs would never hatch, they did—the first four over two days, then two more later. She rejected the last two, but that is another story.

Blanco became a proud, protective mother. She stayed with her chicks for weeks until one day she made it clear she was ready to be out foraging with the other adults. Within no time she started laying eggs again, ready to hatch another brood.

One Sunday, a clear, bright day, the chickens were out in the yard, pecking the ground, rolling in the dust, eyeing us through the windows. I was at the kitchen table when I realized the chickens were clucking as they do when the cat walks by or they become separated. I looked out and saw Stupido and Loco standing calmly beside a bush. The clucking got Leland's attention too, and he headed outside. When he returned much later, he was on the verge of tears. "I can't find Blanco anywhere." The rest of the afternoon was spent first worrying and then mourning, for as the day went on the hope that she had wandered off by herself and would reappear faded. I tried to comfort Leland, but in response to my condolences he said, "I know mom, but it was Blanco."

We all suspected a hawk—her disappearance was so rapid and not even a feather had been left. When I looked out the kitchen window early the next morning with the last glimmer of hope I would see her there, I told myself the story that I would have told a much younger son, "Perhaps she decided to leave with the doves." Perhaps she was the one that got away.

MY FRIDAY NIGHT LIGHTS

A light rain fell on the field. Around me the noise was deafening. Mostly strangers, adorned in caps, t-shirts, and polos in the school colors, huddled under the overhang. I sat in a folding chair behind a folding table and waited for the game to resume, for the crowd to return to the bleachers. The players were called off the field, the spectators out of the stands, because lightening had registered on some sensor.

This was Friday night lights in Texas, to which I was and will remain a stranger albeit I spent years attending football games at the local high school. I had staffed the PTA table for seven of this school's eight years of existence. My older son, Silas, had played football his sophomore year only to gain access to the weight room; my younger son, Leland, now a senior, was a member of the marching band, whose members claimed that football is what happens before and after the halftime show.

It was homecoming night, albeit in the end, the crowning of the royal court was postponed until later, at a dance out of the rain, once the guest team had gone home. Tonight the girls wore tremendous corsages hanging heavily with ribbons and other adornments; the boys wore similar but smaller ones on bands around their arms. The first year we experienced homecoming Silas disappointed his girlfriend because he didn't arrive to school with a corsage. I told him to tell her it was his mother's fault—that she was a "foreigner" and unfamiliar with such traditions. Even more complicated, as a member of the first graduating senior class he was voted a member of the royal court. We had little idea what this meant but managed to get him to the field in a suit. Some of his classmates chanted for him to display his now well-sculpted abs: he pulled up his dress shirt, and they cheered.

I looked at the groups chatting around me. At one time I knew many of the parents, but as Leland aged out of the school system so did I, and I knew fewer and fewer families. I gazed across the field, the light rain visible in the bright lights. Just as I didn't know these parents, they didn't know me. I served on one PTA board or another, sometimes two, for too many years, and I had been on multiple school district committees.

Most germane to my nostalgic glance across the field—recognizing that this school and I were coming to the end of our association—was the extensive investment I made in having this school exist at all. Countless board meetings, several committees, and, closest to my heart, the fight to keep the auditorium when it was almost cut from the budget—all of these hours devoted to what became an organizing principle in the community. It amazed me how the community coalesced around a school, a football team, a band.

But my role in this was the past. I was now an older woman sitting behind the PTA table, trying to sell another t-shirt to help fund senior scholarships, staff luncheons, and the like. As much as I was fading from this community, it was time to let it fade from me. My Friday night lights had come to an end.

THE WORLD OUTSIDE

1968

In the days that followed the 1992 riots in Los Angeles, I found I had little to say. I would mutter some pessimism about us, as a society, never being able to progress forward. Then I found myself thinking about the riots in Brooklyn, when Martin Luther King Jr. was shot.

I was in sixth grade in 1968. I was the only non-Latino White in my classroom—except for the teacher. Of course, back then we didn't say Latino—we said Puerto Rican, Dominican, and the like. I was also the only Jew in the class—again, except for the teacher. And although a classmate might call a woman passing the playground a "white cracker" or curse the Jewish candy store owner, I, just another kid, was exempt from such derision. But as a kid, I also absorbed these confusing messages.

In school we sang "The Ink Is Black," "The House I Live In," and "No Man Is an Island"—all songs that spoke of promised harmony, which I had little reason to doubt; we read success stories about people of every ethnic background, stories that inspired me; and we learned about "liberty and justice for all," to which I pledged. I, trusting as I was, believed every word of it.

The day after Martin Luther King Jr. was shot, my class was on the el, on its way home from a field trip. We had dispersed the length of the car in search of seats. Then, at one stop, students from a local high school poured onto our already crowded car. Word soon reached me that our teacher and Estela, a fair-skinned Puerto Rican girl, had left the train because they were being harassed by the high school students. My friends surrounded me and swore they would protect me; they promised to accompany me all the way home.

Later, my friends "round the corner" said there were to be riots. That night my father stood on the sidewalk in front of our gated store with our two German shepherds; the patrons of the bar next door stopped on their way home and gave him their hearty support. As the night progressed there was shouting, whistling, and sirens, but these were sounds no different from any weekend night.

By the fall of 1968 I lived in a new neighborhood and attended a new school, which was split almost evenly racially. My academically advanced class was all White and mostly Jewish. Many of the Black kids were openly hostile. I felt lost for a long time. I was estranged from a culture I thought familiar and alienated in a culture in which I was naturally grouped.

Through all the conflicts and contradictions of my youth, I was always filled with great hopes and expectations—for an integrated society, a just society, a caring society. Perhaps because I grew up in the midst of that fledgling glimpse of change, I still carry those hopes.

THE DAY THE LIONS STOPPED ROARING

The news of bombings in Brussels in 2016 brought me back to a morning in 1992. I was driving to work and listening to the news. A reporter in Bosnia was giving an update on the siege of Sarajevo. The confusing ethnic–religious war had been dominating the news for months. This morning the reporter told listeners that the roaring of the lions at the Sarajevo Zoo, which had been heard for days amid the gunfire, had stopped. Although no one—I guess he meant no reporter—had gone to check, it was assumed that all the animals had starved. That morning I turned the radio off, and for a long time I closed out news of the Balkans War.

It was not that I cared more about the suffering of animals than that of people. It was the spillover of human violence—humanity's violence—to captured, caged animals, so-called amoral beasts, that I could not abide. It was the utter, senseless cruelty about which I didn't want to hear. It was the pain and suffering I could not bring myself to share.

I once heard about a study of Dutch individuals who had helped Jews escape Nazi Germany. The researchers found that what these people shared was not some moral or social–political conviction but a high degree of empathy. Conversely, when empathy is lacking, we can see others as not like us, and with that view can begin to suspend the moral rules by which we regard ourselves and those like us. One cannot compel empathy, but one can arouse distrust and fear to negate it.

After Brussels there were bombings in Lahore and Baghdad. I know these bombings will not stop in my lifetime. Again and still, here we are, humanity dividing itself into us versus them, committing atrocities in some perverse suspension of moral conduct. Over and over again we prove our inhumanity. Sons and daughters suffer for it, mothers and fathers, brothers and sisters, friends and relations, good people and not-so-good people, and wildlife and animals in zoos.

SEPTEMBER 11

Recently Jim and I attended a birthday party for the about-to-be-eleven-years-old daughter of some friends. Arriving at the party, I was reminded of a similar one for our own sons years ago. We had the party at the same riverside park, where we held several such celebrations. Our boys' birthdays are separated by one month (and five years), so when they were young, we split the difference and held joint parties.

The party scene was not unlike that of our sons' parties, except the children were mostly girls, whereas ours were predominantly boys. Jim and I arrived a bit late; cake just had been served, and faces showed traces of chocolate. A child's voice called out "presents!", and a tight huddle formed around the birthday girl, barely leaving her elbow room as she opened her gifts and the group appraised them. As swiftly as the gifts were opened, once it was a fait accompli, the children ran back to the river.

The river, the Blanco, had more water in it than usual for late summer. Some years we forwent having our sons' party there because the flow was so low we were concerned about water quality. The landscape of the river has changed since those days—two record floods in 2015 scoured much of the banks down to the limestone. Amazingly, a stand of cypresses remained intact. The scene was still beautiful yet a reminder of the power of natural forces.

Just as there were years ago, lots of parents were at the party—parents with infants, parents with school-age children, the grandparents of the birthday girl—family and friends and new school acquaintances enjoying a lovely day at the river.

Of all the parties we had had there, why had I thought of this particular one? Because of the date. I remembered having the party, fifteen years before, a few days after 9/11. Like so many of us, I proceeded through 9/11 in a fog. After reaching my father in Brooklyn immediately after the attack, I could not reach anyone else in my New York family—my mother who lived in lower Manhattan, my sister who worked there, or my brother who lived on the west side with a clear view of the towers. I could not watch the live reports, but I listened to the radio.

I remember Jim and I deliberated with other parents about whether we should cancel the party and decided nothing good would come from doing so; furthermore, we weren't ready to explain the depth of what happened to what would have been disappointed children. I went ahead buying the food, little party favors. And then the day of the party the families came, the adults still numb. We could barely speak, knowing that our world, our children's world, had changed forever. But we all went through the motions. There was playing in the river, a barbecue, birthday cake, the gifts, and before the party was over, the piñata. I am sure we all laughed, as we did every year, about the first birthday party I had hosted in Texas, when I thought piñatas came filled with candy, and the young children were baffled when nothing fell from the enormous hole they had made.

Now a guest, I watched the parents of the birthday girl work to keep the flow of the party going—it is a job, to manage the food, make sure no gifts are lost, make sure no child is left at the river unattended. This party will probably pass unremarked in the memories of these girls, just as that one fifteen years ago has probably joined a blur of river-birthday-party memories in the minds of our boys. Yet it remains with me, when we carried on with everyday life in the face of so much loss.

FINDING HOME

THE SMELL OF FRESH-CUT GRASS

When my first born, Silas, was seven months old, I decided to visit my family of origin. I was feeling somewhat lost in the place I had arrived — motherhood, infants in general, was a foreign territory for me, and I was in a work transition, without a foot in either world.

The trip was an adventure in travel. We boarded a bus in suburban Maryland — mother, child, and the slimmest of supplies in a backpack. My trip was not filled with expectations; I hoped only to survive the journey.

We spent our first day in my mother's neighborhood on the Lower East Side of

Manhattan. Alphabet City, avenues A thru D, was home to a New York blend of Latinos, bohemians, senior citizens, and druggies. On Fourteenth Street, the broad shopping avenue, we bought a cheap stroller and then headed toward the East River Park in search of a playground. Silas was enthralled with the city streets. He wrinkled his nose and snorted at all the passersby. There was so much to see!

We crossed over East River Drive on a walkway littered with glass and garbage. On the strip of grass and asphalt alongside the river, city dwellers took their rest and relaxation—conversation, strolling, jogging, softball. However, the tranquility I typically would find in a large body of water was lost to me.

The playground we sought had been torn up for renovation. As we made our way back across the walkway, dodging large shards of glass and inhaling huge volumes of auto exhaust, my mother said, "I love the smell of fresh-cut grass." I looked around. How she could detect a molecule of this scent?

We made our way to Tompkins Square Park, a 10-acre urban green space with a long history, and found a playground filled with kids and parents of all ages. As my mother swung her grandson in a swing, I chatted with an East Village stylish young couple. We talked about parenting matters, such as baby proofing our respective apartments. We commiserated about the difficulties of finding enough space to move things out of our child's reach. Yet as we talked I realized that not enough space in New York City was another order of magnitude smaller than our two-bedroom apartment. What space could they have? How did they manage?

We carve out a place where we live—a place we eventually call home and which becomes some measure of normal. We find relaxation in a crowded park or smell a blade of grass amid the asphalt.

Returning to the place that first defined my world, I found some grounding in my new life.

THE BOY FROM THE CENTER OF THE UNIVERSE

I met the new graduate student in the stairwell, where I was talking with a professor. He raced up the staircase to learn he had just missed her class. I was taken by his ease with her, his obvious familiarity with the course material.

At the end of the next class, the new guy suggested we all retire to the favorite graduate student beer haunt, and a good group of us did. During the course of the evening I asked him where he was from, and he replied, "The center of the universe." I couldn't decide whether his reply was charming or annoyingly uninformative.

Over the next few weeks I would often meet the new guy on the way to the biology building. He would point out an inconspicuous wildflower and turn its biology into an exciting story of nature. He would direct my attention to a bumblebee, visiting one flower and then its closest neighbor. Because the wildflower's gene dispersal was mediated by this pollinator, if most pollinators visited flowers only in close proximity to one another, the wildflower's genetic neighborhood would be small. Small genetic neighborhood could eventually lead to differentiation among populations of the wildflower, and ultimately, theoretically speaking, speciation.

It turned out the new guy was headed to Virginia over Thanksgiving, close to my own destination, and he offered me a ride. So it was that I arrived at the center of the universe: a town in the Shenandoah Valley with one traffic light, a gas station, a small food market, and few other amenities.

I guess I had grown up thinking I was from the center of the universe. Of course *everyone* in the country—perhaps the world—was interested in New York City: we *were* the advance guard of high culture. With exposure to other places and maturity this attitude wore off, but in ways my family continued to hold me to it for a long time. My mother would talk to me as if I knew of various art events in the city, my father expected me to remember the roadways, and my siblings at times presumed I was still familiar with city politics. They still perceived me as a New Yorker, and its imprint, of course, remains with me.

Eventually, I ended up in Texas, and it would be an understatement to say that Texans see their state as the center of the universe. The word that comes to mind is vainglorious. Texas stars and the state outline are constant decorating motifs, school children say a pledge to the republic along with one to the nation, and many Texans have never traveled beyond Texas' border and have no interest in doing so. There is a postcard I have seen that is reminiscent of the famous *New Yorker* cover showing the coasts with a shrunken wasteland in between; the postcard shows Texas constituting most of the USA and other regions are given names such as "Yankeeland."

I guess there is nothing wrong with thinking your hometown is the center of the universe; the problem arises when you mistake it for the entire universe and cannot fathom that others hold a totally different perspective.

As to that boy from the center of the universe—the one who could find a world in the intimate association of an insect and a plant—I married him.

TOLERANCE LIMITS: AUGUST 9, 2009, 9:30 A.M.

The holly tree outside our kitchen window may die. Its berries are shriveled, its branches spare of leaves. It is twenty years old or more—hard to tell in this harsh environment—but the current drought reveals that it has reached the limits of its tolerance.

I regard the holly as I sip coffee the morning after our return. It is 9:30 a.m. and already well into the nineties. If we had been here, we would have watered it, but we were gone for a month. We, with our mobility, escaped.

I am transplanted outside my native range. At times I feel I am growing older but not flourishing in this soil. Perhaps if I had been transplanted earlier, I would have absorbed the local elements more readily.

Every summer we leave Texas and go home, east, where deciduous trees grow tall, rivers flow, and hot summers are a few days in the nineties. After a month or so, we come back, and I face down the months of prolonged summer.

Some years I am ready to return to my home here, my own life. This year, though, I am overwhelmed by the heat, the powdery dust of the caliche road, the scorching bright light that hurts my eyes.

Jim tells me about an article he has just read. Astronomers have found a way to correct for the turbulence of the Earth's atmosphere in telescopic images and now have crystal clear views of stars in seventy percent of the universe. By taking photos at timed intervals, they are making time-lapse movies of events that occurred billions of years ago, like a star being pulled toward a black hole and then jettisoned out of the galaxy.

My mind is cluttered, too cluttered to focus on innumerable tasks I face, starting today. As much as I hate those broadly circulated emails, there was one that spoke to me, and I try to remember it at times like these: fill your jar first with the three big rocks, then add the smaller ones. Sometimes such a simple directive is a struggle. I close the blinds; the light sears my eyes even inside the house.

I call my older sister as I start to make my post-trip rounds, checking in with the family.

Toward the end of the conversation she returns to a point she cannot get away from lately—now in her mid-fifties, having devoted over twenty years of her life to a state arts agency, having made a home there, she had been fired by an outgoing political appointee. Almost flippantly, he took away her income, her career, her professional network, her life as she has known it. From a working-class background and a city college education she had worked her way up to one of the highest positions there, but it was an apogee susceptible to the vagaries of a political environment. She was jettisoned, with thin explanation, and now she is trying to reconstruct the events that so quickly, so unexpectedly, have aspirated her entire context.

I hope we can rescue our holly. It is a beautiful tree, not particularly uncommon to the Texas Hill Country, but at the edge of its range, its tolerance limits, it is not common either. It seems that for all the tree has survived, one brutally dry summer should not undo its accomplishment. Yet this is the harshness natural forces can exert. It is easier to view them as past events, through a lens corrected for turbulence.

ENDING CHAPTERS

THE UNVEILING

"Do you need to go?" my younger sister asks as we hug hello in front of the cemetery's office. "The bathroom's around the side of the building."

It is 2008, and we are gathering for my father's unveiling, the traditional Jewish ceremony within a year of death during which the newly placed tombstone is literally unveiled of a sheath of cloth. Okay, we pushed the date a little beyond one year, but for my father Judaism was more about habit than a divine system of beliefs.

We linger until most of our group arrives—the route to my father's grave is convoluted—but eventually we are pressed to move on by the cemetery employees managing traffic. A New York cemetery on Sunday suffers internal traffic jams as well as lost souls.

We reassemble graveside and await the stragglers to arrive. My brother's ex greets me, "How was the traffic?"

"Not bad," I reply, not really wanting to talk traffic.

"Whaddidya take?"

"The L.I.E."

"The Southern State was bad," he tells me. "A lot of beach traffic."

My pseudo-stepsister, the daughter of my father's lady friend of twenty years, is talking about her mother's funeral. Like my father's, her mother's body had been wrapped, according to tradition, in gauze. "I always feel like she's looking down on me, saying 'What, you couldn't bury me in a nice pantsuit?'"

Finally, all assembled in our Sabbath best on an unusually hot June day, we begin. Our young, round rent-a-rabbi, sweating profusely, begins with the customary prayers, which none of us understand because they are in Hebrew. Then the man who never knew my father begins to speak of him.

"I have read many words inscribed on tombstones, but I have never seen these particular words. These words tell me much about the man: 'honest, caring, giving.' These words tell me Irving was a real *mensch*. And that is why, a year later, I see such a group willing to *schlep* all the way out here to show their love and respect one more time."

Such a group the rabbi must see: my father's four aging children; my older sister's companion in a wheelchair, partially paralyzed since a stroke; my brother's ex, who has brought his mother; my obviously goy husband. Three of four grandchildren are attendant—their Jewish heritage obviously diluted. My mother has come. My pseudo-stepsister and her husband have brought Mary, the heavily accented, partially deaf woman from Haiti, whom home health care, and perhaps the divine, had sent to my father when his infirmities demanded round-the-clock assistance.

At the end of the service we all scour the ground for a pebble; to place one on the headstone of the deceased is another tradition.

Let this be an important lesson—pebbles in a Jewish cemetery are a hot commodity, so plan ahead and bring one from home.

My younger son, in tears, clings to me.

"Why are you crying?" my mother asks him. "Are you thinking about your own mortality?"

"No mom," I seem to have to explain. "He's sad."

Some of us wander behind my father's stone to visit his parents' graves. Now on a cemetery outing, we decide to visit my father's sister's grave. She passed away only weeks before the unveiling. My two older siblings, who had attended her funeral, head off in opposite directions. I don't know how each of us decides whom to follow—probably a decision borne of proximity—but I follow my older sister.

"He's going the wrong way," she asserts with annoyance. I look over my shoulder and see my brother motioning for us to follow him. "This way," he insists.

Eventually all paths lead to the graves—my aunt, her husband, and their only son. My older son arrives with my brother—he has shed his dress shirt and boasts his sleeveless muscle shirt.

Once back at the cars we rearrange the passengers and all drive a distance to a restaurant–bar that is in view of our old home in Rockaway. We had decided our father would have liked the setting—sitting on a deck over the bay in which he spent hours fishing without success.

My younger sister anxiously rearranges tables to claim them.

My niece maximizes the distance between her and her mother. "I wish she would calm down. She's driving me crazy."

"This is miserable," my brother complains. "How could it be this hot? It's only June."

The heavily accented waitress, more accustomed to drunken diners, grows impatient with our deliberations over the menu. "Whaddayagonnahave?" she prods.

Other guests arrive, most wearing shorts. An old friend refuses to eat; instead, she recounts how she has been violently ill all week from food poisoning. Our oldest guest, in her nineties, has been told we are getting together for a party because funerals make her too sad. She comes up to me, inches from my face, and asks "So what have you been doing to feed your soul?" I lose sight of my younger son and find him at the bar, where I am told he ordered a martini, shaken not stirred. The bartender thinks he is cute, so she has served him a Shirley Temple instead.

The hot afternoon wears on. Finally, all soaked with sweat, a few of us with frayed nerves, we begin to say our farewells.

I don't know what others may think of the rag-tag assembly in remembrance of my father, but I know it would have suited him. He accepted his unconventional, extended family, and he welcomed our friends. He was honest, caring, and giving. A man who struggled to read, who worked with his hands, who scantly made a living, and who spent years with limited mobility and eventually blindness could raise a *minyan* any day of the week of those who truly loved him.

SARAH

"The worst thing that could happen has happened," my younger sister, Sarah, tells me. "I died. I'm dead"

"But if you're dead," I ask her, "how can you be talking to me?"

"I'm in another place. You wouldn't understand," she says. "Nothing matters anymore."

At 52 years, Sarah is one week into hospice care. She has decided she is done with treatment. She is on a steroid to reduce swelling in her brain, but the cancer is wreaking havoc there. In two months she will die.

I don't argue with her, I accept her reality. And I see in what she tells me the truest expression of her anxiety: in her reality the greatest hurdle has come to pass—she is dead, and she no longer has to fear dying.

I go to visit her. There is no other way to say it—I am going to say goodbye. She is barely Sarah anymore, although her dry humor shows itself in flashes. The cancer has eroded her short-term memory. All day long she awakens from a semi-sleep and repeats "I must be out of it. I don't know what's been going on." I tell her she has been sick. Sometimes she rallies and says she is resting to get well. Worse is when she does remember, when she knows she has cancer and is dying. Still, she worries more about her family than herself.

"I guess I've had some bad luck," she says one morning and begins to cry. Later an old friend calls. She tells me how Sarah taught her to think for herself and follow her heart. On the phone, Sarah comes alive, laughing and chatting. Later she tells me she is lucky to have good friends.

Her greatest pleasure is chocolate mousse cake. She wants to go to the grocery, and when we get there she leads me directly to the bakery. Back home she tells me she isn't hungry, but while I am busy elsewhere she serves herself slices of cake.

In a week I am gone. I can think only of the time we didn't spend together, of the opportunities we have missed.

The reality my nieces and brother-in-law live with worsens. Sarah hallucinates more. She begins to refuse her meds, she is agitated, not sleeping, not eating, not talking. Death is painful but merciful for all.

Sarah, living her values, thinking of others, has donated her body for medical research. Her husband holds a small memorial on the West Coast.

On the East Coast her family of origin holds a memorial one month later. We make sure there is chocolate mousse cake on the menu. We tell everyone to enjoy the food, the drink, and the company because that is what Sarah would have wanted. One of Sarah's old friends tells us how Sarah was the one who saved her from her dreadful family life by believing in her and laughing with her in the best and worst of times.

Some days, out of seemingly nowhere, deep grief returns to me. I miss her, and I am sad for the suffering she endured. I try to remember the lessons of those last months of her life, those months of her dying—to lean on my siblings and let them lean on me; to treasure my good friends; to enjoy the indulgence of a rich dessert. But most of all those last months taught me a lesson I have to remind myself of over and over again: to keep things in perspective. Small anxieties are stand-ins for ultimate fears, and we have to face down those fears as bravely as Sarah did the day she said to the doctors, "I'm done."

MY MOTHER'S SONGBOOK

My mother is an encyclopedia of songs—songs of her parents' generation, songs of her own youth, show tunes spanning multiple generations, and the rock and roll of her children's day, albeit the more melodic tunes. She might break out in these songs without warning—some phrase, sight, or smell accessing the library. Sometimes the connection is obvious, sometimes subtle, sometimes a clear window into her subconscious.

My mother's proclivity toward singing no matter the setting used to cause me and my siblings great embarrassment, particularly on those occasions when her subconscious led her to a selection that we found totally inopportune. But sometimes the embarrassment derived solely from her singing in public—not that her voice was poor, but, well, spontaneous public performance, particularly by mothers, was appropriate only in musicals.

A self-described culture-vulture, my mother grew up in small-town New Jersey but was happy to escape to New York City. Until she was ninety-three, she frequented concerts and some smaller music venues, including an "open mic" organized by the widow of one of the well-known New York Ash brothers.

During a visit the spring she was eighty-nine, she told me that "it all goes downhill after ninety." This was my mother's humor and her worry. The infirmities were accumulating, including the memory lapses.

During my visit she sang me songs she remembered and would like to hear played again. She had been searching for the sheet music of one particular song—the very talented pianist at open mic had promised to accompany her. She told me she didn't usually sing at these events because she had lost her singing voice. I asked her if she played her piano at all, and she said she hadn't in a long time.

More than once over the course of my visit she brought up an article I had sent her about the history of a song made famous by the Andrew Sisters, "Bei Mir Bist Du Schoen." She told me the article misspelled the title (the Yiddish would be *Bei Mir Bistu Shein*); that her sister told her a different history of the song, which she preferred to believe; and that when her brother-in-law, returning from the Yiddish theater, first sang the song to her sister, her sister didn't appreciate it because he mistakenly sang it in C major instead of the minor key.

My mother is a songbook. Each song is full of memories. I am no longer embarrassed.

ABOUT THE AUTHOR

Eva Silverfine left New York City at the age of seventeen and arrived in semi-rural Texas at thirty-eight. Between those two points she lived in five other states, earned a BS in Environmental Conservation, an MS in Ecology, worked in a research lab, and combined her background in science with her interest in writing to become a copy editor. In Texas she has raised two sons, freelanced for a variety of academic presses, and continued writing memoir and fiction in the in-between spaces.

Please visit her at www.evasilverfine.com.